Cambridge English Readers

....

Level 5

Series editor: Philip Prowse

Dolphin Music

Antoinette Moses

T0134247

CAMBRIDGE
UNIVERSITY PRESS

CAMBRIDGE
UNIVERSITY PRESS

University Printing House, Cambridge CB2 8BS, United Kingdom

One Liberty Plaza, 20th Floor, New York, NY 10006, USA

477 Williamstown Road, Port Melbourne, VIC 3207, Australia

314–321, 3rd Floor, Plot 3, Splendor Forum, Jasola District Centre, New Delhi – 110025, India

79 Anson Road, #06–04/06, Singapore 079906

Cambridge University Press is part of the University of Cambridge.

It furthers the University's mission by disseminating knowledge in the pursuit of education, learning and research at the highest international levels of excellence.

www.cambridge.org
Information on this title: www.cambridge.org/9780521666183

© Cambridge University Press 1999

First published 1999
Reprinted 2018

Printed in the United Kingdom by Hobbs the Printers Ltd

A catalogue record for this publication is available from the British Library

ISBN 978-0-521-66618-3 Paperback

Contents

Characters

Saul Grant: writer and music critic.

Caroline Fry: musician, Saul's girlfriend.

Ruth Hunter: member of PACE.

Sue Hunter: Ruth's granddaughter, also a member of PACE.

Captain Marrs: head of BEATCON, an anti-terrorist organisation.

Dick Lane: a BEATCON special officer.

The Controller: head of Control, the ruling government of Europe.

Peter: the Controller's brother.

Wind: a dolphin.

Marc: a member of PACE.

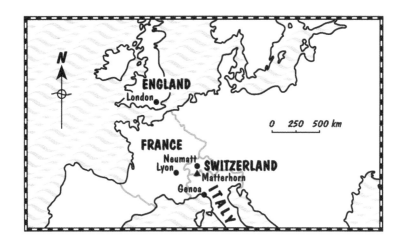

Chapter 1 *Life was good*

Tuesday 27 May, 2051. 2 p.m. Richmond, England.

'We have been working on blue with black letters for three hours, five minutes and twenty five seconds.' Saul Grant's computer spoke with a Scottish accent. 'We will now change to black and white for one hour.'

'OK,' Saul told the machine. He yawned and rubbed his red eyes. He had been working for too long today. His computer knew that. His computer knew everything. It knew Saul's voice and Saul could talk to it if he wanted to.

But he did not like talking to his computer. He liked writing and found it difficult to think and talk at the same time. He did not know why, but he did know that many of the Web writers had the same problem.

Saul Grant was a writer. He was a music critic for the Central England Web Guide. He loved music and he loved writing about music. Many people wanted his job, but he was good at it and his bosses were pleased with him.

But next week he had to stop writing and do six months of community work. Saul hated community work.

Everyone had to do it. Saul knew that. There were too many people and too few jobs. Today, no-one was allowed to work for more than one year without a break, except for those working for Control. Control managers worked every year. But then Control made the rules. Control ruled the Web. Control ruled everything. Control was short for Control Europe Ltd. It had replaced all other European governments.

And what Control said about community work made sense. Someone had to look after the old people. Today, more than three-quarters of the population of Europe was over seventy years old and needed someone to look after them. So all young people under thirty had to help the old people. Saul hated it. He wanted to stay at home and write about new music.

Today most new music was written by dolphins. And dolphin music was beautiful. Only five years ago they had discovered that dolphins could not only sing, but could actually write music. And now they had taken dozens of dolphins to recording studios, so that everyone could hear their music on the Web. Every dolphin had a quite different song and could write music that sounded as individual as the music written by people. But it was so much better, thought Saul. It was wonderful. He loved listening to dolphin music and enjoyed writing about it.

Saul leaned back in his chair and switched his windows open. It was another burning hot summer day outside. You could not go outside without wearing a helmet or eye mask and special anti-reflection material, called anti-glare. No-one could work outside – the countryside was now almost empty – and it was very expensive to put anti-glare on cars or over gardens.

Most transport was by jet power and wind power and people only travelled when they had to. People lived in small groups of houses and everything was delivered through the tunnels. When you did go out, you always had to tell Control where you were going and why.

Once, Saul knew, people had enjoyed walking in the countryside. They had climbed mountains and swum in the sea. Today everyone went virtual travelling in their exercise rooms. You put on a helmet or mask and chose where you wanted to go, and then the type of sport, and there you were. One day you could be water skiing in the Indian Ocean and the next day you could be walking in Tibet, in the Himalayas.

The virtual world is a happy world, as Control said, and Saul was happy; he enjoyed his work and his life, he met interesting people at virtual concerts and he had a wonderful girlfriend.

Her name was Caroline Fry. She played the cello in the Europafest Confederation Orchestra and she lived and worked in Neumatt, Switzerland. She and Saul would get together on the Web most nights and talk, and at weekends, when they were not busy, they would go on virtual walks and holidays together. He had never actually touched Caroline. But virtual touching was fun. You could be with the person you loved and imagine what it felt like to touch them. When Saul and Caroline got married, they would meet, of course. But at the moment they both enjoyed their lives. The Web controlled their lives, but that was how things were.

'You've never had it so good,' said the screen every night before it switched itself off.

And, listening to the dolphin music in his comfortable house, Saul would think that Control was right, that life today was good.

Chapter 2   *PACE*

Monday 2 June, 2.30 p.m. Richmond.

Mrs Ruth Hunter was the third and last of Saul's old people that day. But it did not seem that she needed very much help. She was quite able to use the computer, to do her own shopping, cleaning and cooking. She was a bright, lively woman with a loud laugh. Saul liked her, but there was something about her that he was not sure about. She was different.

'Come and sit down, Saul,' said Ruth. 'There's something I need to tell you.'

Saul sat down. Old people often told him things about themselves and about the past, but they usually said things like, 'Have I told you about the time when ... ?' or 'I was a great beauty once, you know ...' This was different. Ruth Hunter sounded more like his computer.

'Saul,' asked Ruth Hunter. 'Do you like dolphins?'

'What a strange question,' thought Saul.

'Yes,' he replied. 'Of course I like dolphins.'

'We've read what you've written about dolphin music,' Ruth continued, which answered the question he was about to ask. 'And that's why we've chosen you.'

We? Chosen? Saul did not understand.

'You didn't choose me,' he said. 'The computer chose *you* as one of the three old people I visit this month.'

'No, dear,' replied Ruth Hunter. 'I wasn't on your original list. But we managed to change it on the Web.'

'What!' Saul could not believe what she was saying. This was crazy. Perhaps she was crazy. And who was the 'we' she kept talking about.

'We,' continued Ruth. She again answered his question before he had time to ask it. 'We are a group of what you call old people. But we do not feel old. And we're angry. We're very angry at the way the world is now ruled by Control. And we want to change it.'

'You're not allowed to say things like that!' Saul was shocked. 'Everything Control does is for the best. Think about it! There are no wars any more and no pollution. It's not for us to criticise Control.'

Ruth laughed. It was a big laugh. 'I'm old enough, dear, to say what I like. And I'm not alone. There are a great many people who don't agree with Control.'

'You don't say things like that to other people, do you?' asked Saul. 'You mustn't do that. They'll take you away from this nice house and send you to the Education Rooms.' Saul rather liked Ruth even though she was clearly crazy. He did not want the police to take her away. And it would not be good for him, either. After all, he was supposed to be looking after her.

'Yes, I do say what I think,' said Ruth. 'But don't worry. I don't say it on the Web. There is a small group of us. We have ways of sending each other information. The police won't take me to the tunnels. That is, in fact, where they take people, Saul. The tunnels. The Education Rooms don't exist. They were created on a computer. But we won't be going to the tunnels, we know how to avoid the police.'

'You keep saying "we". Who are "we"?' asked Saul.

Ruth looked at him. 'I am telling you this because I think you are a good man. I think you have a great deal to learn, but your heart is good. You must not tell anyone else about this. If you tell anyone, even your girlfriend Caroline, then they really will kill me.'

'You're joking,' said Saul. Then he asked, 'How do you know about Caroline? I haven't told you about her.'

'From the Web,' said Ruth. 'We don't use the Web to talk to each other but we can use it in many other ways.'

This was getting too much for Saul. 'But it's not allowed. You really should stop this. If Control finds out, you'll be in big trouble.'

'Saul, dear, please don't talk to me as if I were a small child. I'm old, but I'm not stupid. I know exactly how dangerous this is. They've shot many of my friends already. Please sit down,' she said as Saul stood up. 'What I am saying is the truth. And I need you to listen to what I have to say. We have decided that you are the man to help us.'

Saul sat down again. He needed to sit down. He could not believe what he was hearing.

'But who are "we"?' he asked again.

'We,' said Ruth, 'are a group of people who can remember the world before Control. We call ourselves PACE. That stands for People Against Control in Europe. Control, however, calls us terrorists.'

'You're terrorists?' Saul put his face in his hands.

This was not happening to him. He wanted to be back in his room listening to music. He did not want to be here talking to a nice old lady who he suddenly discovered was a terrorist. This was impossible. Old people working against Control. This was really crazy.

'PACE is not a violent group,' said Ruth. 'But we do work with some other European groups who prefer direct methods.'

'Direct methods?' wondered Saul.

'Bombs, setting fire to Control centres, that kind of thing,' replied Ruth with a smile.

Saul began to ask himself if any of this was true. Perhaps it was all in Ruth's head. Perhaps she thought that she was part of a group, but in fact there was no group at all. Yes, that was it. A few old people met and imagined that they were terrorists. Perhaps they were remembering the kind of thing that happened when they were young. Perhaps they just wanted to live in the past. Saul smiled.

'How do you communicate?' Saul asked. 'I thought that it was impossible to avoid the Web Control.'

'Of course it is,' said Ruth. 'You can't avoid Control if you use the Web. PACE uses the Web to get information, but it doesn't communicate with its members on the Web.'

'I see,' said Saul. He was right. This was just an imaginary group.

'No,' said Ruth. 'You don't see at all. You think I'm a crazy old lady and I'm imagining all of this. You think that I've invented PACE. You think that tonight you'll go home and laugh about it.' She laughed herself. 'But I'm not crazy and PACE does exist.'

Ruth Hunter took out a large book from her shelf.

'Oh no,' thought Saul, 'a photograph album. She is going to show me pictures of herself when she was young and tell me how wonderful it was.'

Ruth opened the album. 'Look at these pictures,' she said. 'They were taken a month ago.'

'A month ago ...' began Saul. 'How ... ? Who ... ? No-one takes photographs today ...'

'How and who doesn't matter,' said Ruth. 'What is important, what does matter is the photographs themselves.'

Saul looked at the pictures. They were of glass tanks, like big fish tanks. But there were electric wires, lots of wires coming from the tanks. And inside the tanks was water and something else. Was it a laboratory?

'What are they?' he asked.

'Dolphins,' said Ruth. 'These are dolphins in a terrible place called the Music Rooms. These dolphins are making music. They are hurting the dolphins to make music.'

'Hurting ...' repeated Saul. It still did not make sense.

Ruth explained. 'When they are happy, dolphins do not make music. They make sounds yes, many kinds of taps and whistles, but not music, not the kind of music you have been writing about.'

'I don't understand,' said Saul. 'I've seen the dolphins playing in huge pools. They all look happy.'

'Those are different dolphins. How can you tell the difference? You can't talk to them.'

'No,' Saul agreed. 'But why would anyone do this?'

'Money,' said Ruth. 'Everyone is buying dolphin music.'

'But how do dolphins make music, then?' asked Saul.

'Do you know what a swan song is?' asked Ruth.

'No,' replied Saul.

'When I was young, people thought that when a swan died, it sang. In its very last moments it could sing. I think that later they found out that this wasn't true about swans, but people still used the expression to mean the last great thing you do before you die. But it is actually true about dolphins. When they are in terrible pain and dying, they sing. Just before they die, they make a song that is the most wonderful music in the world and that is their swan song.'

'But dolphins enjoy making music. I know they do.'

'You have been told that dolphins enjoy making music. It's not true. To get the dolphins to make music, they take the dolphins and put them into these small glass tanks only just bigger than the dolphins themselves. That itself is terrible for the animals. They are in pain if they can't move. But then to make it worse, they put electricity through them. When the dolphins think they are dying, they begin to sing. And men record them.'

'No!' shouted Saul. 'It can't be true!' Saul was furious. How dare Ruth say these things. 'I don't believe it.'

Saul stood up. 'You're crazy!' he told Ruth. 'I came here to look after you, and you talk to me about terrorists, and now you try to tell me that dolphins don't enjoy making music. I know dolphin music. I listen to it every day. I write about it. It's the most beautiful music in the world. I've had enough of this. I'm going home.'

Saul ran out of the house and got into his electric car. 'The woman is mad, the woman is mad; it's not true, it's not true,' he repeated to himself, as his car took him along the road back home.

Chapter 3 *Cello suite*

Monday 2 June, 6 p.m. Richmond.

Saul was still furious when he got home. He went straight to his computer.

'Welcome home, Saul,' said the computer. 'Do you wish to work on the Web now or would you like your messages? There is a message waiting for you from Caroline.'

It was all so familiar, it was home. This was the world he knew. What had happened this afternoon wasn't real. It couldn't have been real. It was just a mad old woman and her fantasies.

'My messages first, please,' said Saul. He sat back in his comfortable chair. A face appeared on his computer screen. It was a young woman. She had obviously made the message in a hurry. She was wearing a dressing gown and was drying her hair with a towel. Her long dark hair fell over her shoulders and hid half of her face. Beside her, on a chair, was her cello and she was also studying her laptop computer, which showed lines of music. Beside the computer were piles of printed music and she seemed to be comparing the printed music to the examples on the screen.

She looked up at the screen as if she was surprised that the camera was there, as if she had already forgotten that she was sending a message. 'Caroline always does that,' thought Saul. It was one of the many little things about her that he found both attractive and annoying.

'Oh Saul, darling,' said Caroline. 'I'm here at home for a few hours before my concert. It's now five o'clock European time and I'm not going out again until about eight o'clock. But then I will be out till late, I expect. The orchestra is giving a party for Peggy, you know, the one who plays first violin, the one with the grey hair. The one you always say looks like a rabbit. You're so naughty! Anyway, she's sixty years old now, so she has to retire. Poor old thing, she cried at the end of yesterday's concert. Do phone me for a chat. I haven't seen you for days. Well, two days, but it seems much longer. I hope the PODs haven't driven you crazy yet. Miss you! Love you! Bye!'

PODs meant 'Poor Old Dears' and was Caroline's private language. She called all old people PODs. Caroline liked to invent words. It was one of her methods of escaping from the way life was controlled. Inventing words and through her music.

'When I play,' she once told Saul, 'I am in control. No-one controls me.'

'If only I could tell Caroline everything about Ruth Hunter,' thought Saul. He wanted very much to tell Caroline, but he was not sure how she would react. Perhaps she would laugh at him, or would she just be angry that he had believed the old woman? 'But you weren't there,' argued Saul in his head. And then he wondered why he was arguing with Caroline on behalf of Ruth. Did that mean that he believed Ruth? Was it true about the dolphins?

'Call Caroline,' Saul told his computer.

Caroline appeared on the screen. She was now wearing a

loose red cotton dress and her long hair was tied back with what looked like a piece of string. She was playing her cello and continued to play even after she had agreed to take the call. Saul watched her with pleasure. She was so beautiful with her pale skin and green eyes that he never got tired of looking at her. He loved the way her neck bent as she played. And she played so beautifully. He recognised the music as a Bach cello suite, one of Caroline's favourite pieces of music. She's playing it at her next concert, he thought. He waited until she had finished playing before he spoke.

'That was wonderful,' Saul told her.

'Thank you, darling,' said Caroline. 'It's so nice to have one's own personal critic.' Caroline laughed. 'How are you?' she asked.

'Fine,' said Saul.

'How are the PODs?'

'Shall I tell her?' wondered Saul.

'Darling,' asked Caroline, 'are you listening to me? I enquired how your PODs were today? You have spent today with PODs, haven't you? How were they?'

'There was one, my last one of the day,' said Saul. 'She's called Ruth and she's not very old. She's rather lively, really. So I didn't have very much to do.'

'Oh, lucky old you. I've had an exhausting day.'

'She was very strange actually,' continued Saul. He stopped. Ruth had told him not to tell anyone but ... 'Caroline?' Saul began.

'Yes, darling,' she answered, singing quietly to herself.

'Have you ever heard of the Music Rooms?' Saul asked.

'The what?' replied Caroline.

'A place called the Music Rooms,' continued Saul.

'No, I've never heard of it,' replied Caroline.

'It's where they keep the dolphins,' explained Saul. 'It should be quite near you. It's somewhere in the Neumatt Arts Centre.'

'Really, Saul, I don't know what you're talking about,' Caroline frowned. 'I mean, I play in rehearsal rooms and practise in practice rooms. And they are all here in the Neumatt Arts Centre. But I've never heard any of them called the Music Rooms. And I live here. Why are you asking me this?'

How much did he dare tell her? 'Oh,' he said. 'It's nothing. Just a name I heard recently.'

'Dolphin music just gets better and better, doesn't it?' said Caroline, who was obviously not curious about the name of a room. 'Did you hear that new piece by Wind?' she asked. 'Wasn't it wonderful?'

'Yes,' agreed Saul. 'It was marvellous. Caroline,' he began again, 'do you think that dolphins enjoy making music?'

'Of course they do, otherwise they wouldn't do it.' Caroline sounded annoyed. 'You're in a very strange mood today, Saul. Are you depressed? What's the matter with you? Have you been drinking?'

'No,' said Saul. 'No, it's nothing. Just a long day. I'm tired. Just the usual odd thoughts.'

'Well, they don't sound like your usual thoughts at all. I've never known you to ask so many questions. I don't think I like it very much. What's this Ruth woman been saying to you? Did you get these ideas from her? You know how old-fashioned PODs are, Saul. They don't like anything that's different from when they were young. And you still haven't asked me about how my recording went or wished me luck for tonight's concert.'

'I'm sorry,' said Saul. 'I wasn't thinking. Do tell me how the recording went. I want to know.'

'OK,' said Caroline, happier now the conversation was about music. She told Saul about the problems she was having with a new sonata. Saul listened and offered advice and encouragement. He promised Caroline that he would watch her next virtual concert, in two days' time.

'I know you will,' said Caroline. 'I love you.'

'I love you, too,' said Saul, but he was not really thinking about Caroline. He was wondering whether he dare try once again to tell her what Ruth had said, but then thought that if Caroline didn't know about the Music Rooms, then she would not believe that they existed. If they did exist!

'Must go,' Caroline was saying. 'Love you,' she repeated.

'Love you, too,' Saul agreed. They blew kisses at each other and said goodnight. But after Caroline had gone and he was alone with his computer, Saul sat full of thought in the dark, listening to the new music by the dolphin, Wind. It was so beautiful, unlike any other kind of music. It took you on a journey.

'But what if Ruth is right?' he thought. 'What if this dolphin was about to make his final journey when he made this music, was about to die?'

Saul found that tears were running down his cheeks.

'I have to know,' he thought. 'I'll go back to Ruth tomorrow and I'll find out the truth about the Music Rooms.'

Chapter 4   *BEATCON*

Monday 2 June, 7 p.m. London.

The phrase 'Music Rooms' had an alarm attached to it. So the moment that Saul said the words, his and Caroline's conversation was immediately recorded by BEATCON, the British and European Anti-Terrorist Control Organisation.

The building where BEATCON was based, or B Centre as it was known, was not a beautiful building, but it contained everything that any member of BEATCON had ever wanted. There were the latest Web computers for taking virtual trips and playing games. There was a large swimming pool and gym where BEATCON units could exercise. And there were the latest jetcars and jetbikes which BEATCON officers were allowed to use.

Members of BEATCON were not allowed to get married, but they didn't mind that. They had virtual relationships. And when they were thirty years old, they were offered other jobs. You had to be young in BEATCON. And you had to keep fit. The members of BEATCON were all very fit. There were frequent competitions among the units. And the winners became part of Captain Marrs' special unit. Every BEATCON member wanted to be in the special unit. The competition was tough. And those in the special unit, the specials, were very proud to be there. The specials thought they were the best.

Dick Lane was a BEATCON special and Dick Lane thought that he was the best. He was nineteen years old and had been a member of BEATCON for a year and a special for three months. He exercised in the gym every day for an hour and swam for an hour before he went to bed.

Dick Lane listened to Saul and Caroline. He decided immediately that he didn't like them. They were soft, he thought. They talked about music and things like that. What did Saul do that was any use to anyone? Nothing. He wrote about music. And they were terrorists. Saul knew about the Music Rooms. 'Well,' thought Dick, 'Captain Marrs will know what to do with Saul Grant.'

Dick recorded a copy of Saul and Caroline's conversation and took it to Captain Marrs. Captain Marrs was the head of BEATCON. Very few people knew his name, but those who did never spoke it without a certain amount of fear. Dick Lane thought Captain Marrs was wonderful. He wanted to be just like him.

Captain Marrs watched the conversation. While he watched he drew a picture of Saul's head on a piece of paper. 'Who is this young man who's asking about the Music Rooms?' Captain Marrs wondered. 'Where did Saul Grant hear about the Music Rooms? Who has he been talking to? I shall soon find out,' he said to himself.

He took the picture of Saul's head and stuck it to the wall. Then, taking a laser gun from his belt, he shot through the middle of it. It was a little game he played with every new terrorist that he discovered. He found it amusing.

Although he did not know it, in another room, in

another building, another man was watching Captain Marrs on a screen. The head of Control for Europe, the Controller, had many ways of watching people. In his office, in the Control Centre, he watched everyone. He was the spider at the centre of the web. He knew everything that went on. He controlled everything. The Controller sat in a large, soft chair in his office. It was dark blue, like the walls of his office. There was little light in the room except the light that came from all the screens. The Controller was surrounded by screens.

And at this moment, on one of the screens, the Controller was watching Captain Marrs.

'Marrs is quite mad,' the Controller thought to himself, shaking his head. 'Look at him!' He wondered whether now was the time he should do something about Captain Marrs. Sooner or later, he thought, this man was going to create some real problems for him. Last year Marrs had caused a major fire which burned down a group of houses. And just last week Marrs had blown up a house where a group of young men were having a party. His specials had killed everyone in the house. They thought the men were part of a terrorist group, and it was forbidden for a group of ten or more people to gather in one place without a licence.

Later the Controller found out that the group were only celebrating somebody's birthday and they had forgotten to get a licence. The Controller had to make a statement on the Web saying that another terrorist group had killed the men.

The Controller sighed. He didn't like Marrs' way of doing things, but he also knew that Marrs was valuable to

Control. As head of BEATCON, Marrs had discovered and broken up several organised terrorist groups in the region. It was true that sometimes innocent people died, but there was always a price to pay.

The Controller pressed a button and Marrs' file came up on a screen. Marrs was a man created by the system, the Controller thought as he read the file.

Marrs had joined the army when he was only eighteen, but did very well. He was very quick and very keen. The Controller knew that anyone who blocked Marrs disappeared. The first case the Controller knew about was when a man who was Marrs' senior officer came to see him. The officer wanted to get rid of Marrs because he was scared of him. He was a senior officer, but he was shaking.

That was five years ago, when the Controller first came across Marrs. The officer had had an accident soon after and Marrs took his place. And there were other similar cases, but the Controller could see that Marrs also followed orders, that he wasn't a danger to Control. That's why he had become the head of BEATCON.

The Controller read in the file how Marrs' father and twin brother were both killed by a terrorist bomb in London when Marrs was three years old. His mother went mad after that and, two years later, when Marrs was just five, she threw herself off the roof of a building. Marrs saw her do it. The Controller could understand why Marrs hated all terrorists so much.

That's why he was the perfect head of BEATCON, the Controller thought. He knew he'd never find anyone else so determined, so cruel. So useful.

For the moment, the Controller decided, he would do nothing about Marrs. He would just keep an eye on him.

The Controller turned and looked again at the screen with Captain Marrs on it. Marrs was still shooting at the picture of Saul Grant's head.

'I don't know who Marrs is shooting at,' the Controller said to himself, 'but I don't think he'll be alive for very much longer.'

Chapter 5 *This is crazy!*

Tuesday 3 June, 8 a.m. Richmond.

'You're telling me what?' Saul was almost shouting.

'You're telling me that there are eight dolphins locked up in a mountain in Neumatt, Switzerland and you want me to go there and rescue them. Are you crazy? How am I going to do that?'

'You'll think of something,' said Ruth.

It was the next day. Saul had got up early. He had slept badly and when he did finally fall asleep, he dreamed of dolphins. They were swimming in the sea, but the sea was red with blood and they were calling his name. He had woken up covered in sweat and shaking. He had arrived at Ruth's house in a very bad mood.

To his surprise she was not alone.

'This is Sue,' Ruth said. 'Sue is my granddaughter.'

Saul saw an attractive, slim young woman, with short red hair. She was dressed in black and was sitting in front of a laptop computer, tapping the keys very fast.

'Hi,' Saul said to her. She ignored him and continued to tap for a while, then finally turned to him.

'Look at this,' she said. She didn't seem to bother with 'hello' or 'how nice to meet you', thought Saul. He thought she was extremely rude.

'What is it?' sighed Saul.

'It's the Neumatt Arts Centre. I managed to get in

through the back door. There's always a way to get into these places if you know how. But this place is really hard to get into.'

'Sue is obviously very proud of this,' thought Saul. And he was curious. He looked at the screen. There were two small glass tanks like those in the photographs Ruth had shown him yesterday, but these were being pushed along a corridor. 'This is live,' Saul thought. 'This is now. Sue has managed to get into the cameras on the ceiling. I am watching what is happening in Neumatt Arts Centre at this moment.'

'Hold on a moment,' said Sue. She tapped another few keys. 'It's difficult. I have to keep changing codes in order to follow the dolphins.'

Saul couldn't see anything at first, but then he saw them. Two dolphins in two glass tanks that were far too small for them. The dolphins were trying to move, but were unable to do so. They banged their backs against the lids of the boxes again and again. The sound echoed down the corridor. Saul could hear it clearly. He felt sick.

Sue changed cameras. Now they were inside a room. Saul could see people moving about. They put metal things on one of the dolphins. Someone turned on a switch. The dolphin jumped into the air again and again, and then it stopped. Then the music began. It was so beautiful and so terrible. The dolphin was crying.

Saul found that he was crying too. 'You knew about this?' he asked Ruth.

'Yes,' replied Ruth. 'We've been trying to find out for a long time, but Sue has only just managed to get into the Neumatt Web. It's taken her months and months to find the way in.'

'Do the dolphins die afterwards?' Saul asked. 'After the music?'

'Sometimes they do,' answered Ruth. 'But sometimes they are sent back into the big pools to recover. And then they put them into the Music Rooms again. And because the pain is worse the second time, their song is even longer.'

'I can't believe it,' Saul cried. 'I thought that dolphin music was so beautiful, but it's terrible. I'll never write about dolphin music again, I promise you. Is that why you wanted to talk to me?'

'Saul,' called Sue, before Ruth could reply. 'Come here a minute!'

'Who gave this woman the right to order me about?' thought Saul. He decided that he did not like her at all. But he walked over to where she was sitting and looked into her laptop. He saw a door. There was a red triangle on the door and a sign said:

PRIVATE KEEP OUT.

'It's the entrance to the Music Rooms,' Sue told him. 'The door has a special lock which reads your eyes. It only lets in the people who have permission. You can't break a lock like that. But the memory bank of the lock must be here somewhere.' She continued to tap the keys of the computer.

'You can't do that,' objected Saul. 'It's against the law.'

'So is hurting dolphins,' said Sue sharply.

Saul sighed again. He had never met anyone like this woman before. He watched her. She was not beautiful, Saul thought. Not like Caroline. Sue was too thin, all elbows and knees, and her hair was cut almost as short as a boy's.

Her face was odd, too. Her eyes and her mouth seemed too big for her face.

But he had to admit that he liked her energy, the way she worked. He had never seen anyone use the Web as she did. Her hands moved over the keys like a pianist's. She clearly knew exactly what she was doing.

'Go over there,' Sue ordered Saul, 'and look into the camera.'

'Why . . . ?' began Saul.

'Be quiet and just do it,' said Sue. 'Fine,' she said, a minute later. 'You can look away now.'

Saul looked at the screen of her laptop and found his own face staring back at him. Sue zoomed into his face until just his eyes were visible.

'I'm scanning in your eyes,' she said, 'so that I can put them into the Music Rooms' memory bank. When I've finished, you'll be able to walk into the Music Rooms without any problems.'

'I'll be able to do *what*?' Saul gasped in horror.

'Walk into the Music Rooms,' answered Ruth. 'You're going to rescue the dolphins and take them to the sea. That's the reason I brought you here.'

That was the moment when Saul began to shout.

'Don't you know that Switzerland doesn't have a sea?' Saul demanded. 'Don't you know that the Neumatt Arts Centre is inside the Matterhorn? And the Matterhorn is one of the highest mountains in Europe. Have you thought about that? How on earth can I get dolphins across the Matterhorn to the sea?'

'I know that Switzerland doesn't have a sea,' replied Ruth. 'You don't have to tell me that. I know that the whole idea seems crazy. But we can't leave the dolphins there, can we? You saw them. In any case, Sue will probably find a way,' added Ruth.

'Sue?' repeated Saul.

'Yes,' said Ruth. 'She's going with you. I wouldn't expect you to go on your own.'

Saul shook his head. This was getting crazier and crazier. He had thought for a moment that he might be able to get to Neumatt. He could ask for permission to visit Caroline and ask her to marry him. He had been thinking of doing this for some time. He would be certain to get permission. But to take Sue, who was clearly a terrorist, and had the ability to break into private Web controls . . .

'Absolutely not,' said Saul. 'No, I'm not going. And I'm certainly not going anywhere with Sue.'

'Don't be so silly, dear,' said Ruth. 'You'll need her.'

'No,' said Saul. 'I know that she's your granddaughter, but I can't allow myself to work with a terrorist. I'm sorry.'

Saul turned to Sue. Sue was not listening. She was watching the window.

'Damn,' she swore. 'It's lucky you were early, Saul. They've arrived.'

'Who, dear?' enquired Ruth.

'BEATCON,' said Sue.

'We'd better move then,' said Ruth, calmly.

'BEATCON?' asked Saul, in horror. 'Here? What have you got me into?'

Sue watched the window. 'It's bad,' she said. 'Marrs himself is here. We must move.'

'But I'm not a terrorist,' said Saul. 'I'm meant to be here.

BEATCON won't be interested in me. I'll go and talk to them.'

'You don't talk to Captain Marrs,' said Ruth quietly.

'Who's Captain Marrs?' asked Saul.

'The most evil man in Europe,' said Sue. She pointed out of the window. 'Watch.'

Saul saw a dozen men in black leather climbing out of a large jetcar. They were led by a tall man with a bald head.

'Now watch this,' said Sue. She tapped some keys on her laptop and Saul saw his own car start up.

'What are you doing?' he shouted at Sue.

Saul's car moved forwards slowly along the road. Captain Marrs turned round. He pointed a laser gun and the car exploded into a thousand small pieces.

'Now do you believe me?' demanded Sue. 'When Captain Marrs comes for you, he doesn't stop to make conversation. Now are you coming, or do you want to end up like your car?'

Chapter 6 *Escape*

Tuesday 3 June, 9.15 a.m. Richmond.

'Hurry up!' said Sue. 'Captain Marrs will be here at any moment. Come on,' she insisted. 'Hurry!'

Saul continued to look in horror at the remains of his car. 'He thought I was in that car,' he said. 'Captain Marrs thought I was in my car and he blew it up!'

'Yes, yes,' said Sue impatiently. 'Captain Marrs is like that. Blowing up cars is just the kind of thing he enjoys. Now move. He may blow up this house next.'

Saul did not know if his legs could move. Ruth took him by the shoulders and pushed him out of the room.

'Come along, Saul dear,' she said. 'I know that you're shocked, but we really don't have any time to waste.'

'If this is how Saul behaves when a car is blown up, he's going to be useless on the journey,' Sue complained.

'Don't be too hard on him,' said Ruth. 'I know that you're used to things like this, but for Saul it's all quite new. He's never seen BEATCON in action before. He's never met Captain Marrs. He's never seen a car blown up. The first time is always very frightening.'

They were in the kitchen now.

'Where are we going?' asked Saul in a panic.

'You'll see,' said Ruth. She opened a door in the floor that led down to a tunnel. Sue's laptop computer was small enough and light enough to put in a secret pocket inside her jacket. She put it in and straightened her jacket. Then she stepped on to a ladder and started to climb down. Saul followed her. He moved slowly as if he was in a dream. He felt that his legs and arms were not his. Ruth followed him. She continued to talk to Sue over his head. This made him feel even more that he was not there.

'He'll soon get used to it,' said Ruth. 'I think I was right to choose him. He's not stupid. And he knows people in Neumatt.'

'Well, I hope you're right,' Sue continued to complain. 'But if he doesn't learn quickly, then he's just going to be a danger to both of us.'

'They're talking about me as if I wasn't here,' thought Saul. 'But then I feel as if I'm not here. This is all a bad dream. This isn't happening. Things like this don't happen to me.'

They came to a long tunnel between the houses. To Saul's surprise a man was there.

'I was getting worried,' the man said. Then he lifted one of the stones of the floor of the tunnel. Underneath was another ladder leading down.

'Captain Marrs will guess we came down here,' said Ruth. 'But he doesn't know about this other ladder and I don't think he'll find it, either.'

'No,' said the man. 'He won't have a lot of time to look for you. I telephoned for help. The Controller wasn't very pleased when I told him that Captain Marrs was here. He said he'd come here right away.'

'Well done, Peter!' said Ruth.

'Good luck, my dear,' said the man called Peter.

'Who is he?' wondered Saul. 'Someone very important if

he knows the Controller,' he thought.

'Good luck all of you,' said Peter. 'Don't worry about Captain Marrs. When I shut this stone, no-one will ever know that it was moved. And Marrs won't bother me.' Peter laughed. 'Be careful,' he added. 'I'll send a message that you're on your way after Marrs has gone.'

Saul, Ruth and Sue began to climb down. This ladder went deeper, thought Saul, than any ordinary ladder. Much deeper. It felt very cold. They all climbed down slowly and carefully.

'Who was that man?' asked Saul.

'He's a neighbour,' said Ruth. 'Peter is a very old friend of mine. He used to be a judge.'

'Isn't he in danger staying there?' asked Saul. 'What if Captain Marrs questions him?'

'Oh, I don't think that Captain Marrs will question Peter,' Ruth said. 'Peter is the Controller's younger brother. The Controller is very fond of him. He'll make sure that Peter is all right.'

Saul, Ruth and Sue climbed down and down. The ladder seemed to go on for ever. Saul felt again that he was asleep, in a bad dream that was going on and on. He half heard Ruth talking about the fact that the tunnel had once been a mine. But all he could think about was his car. The way it exploded. The fact that he could have been inside it.

'Thank heavens we've escaped from Captain Marrs,' Saul sighed.

'You must be joking,' said Sue. 'We've escaped this time. But Captain Marrs will be looking for us. This is only the beginning.'

Chapter 7 *Inside the blue helicopter*

Tuesday 3 June, 9.30 a.m. Richmond.

At the same moment that Peter was helping Saul, Ruth and Sue down on to the ladder, a small, blue and silver helicopter landed outside Ruth's house. The Controller stepped out and looked around him.

He saw the remains of Saul's car and the BEATCON soldiers who had now lined up and were preparing to attack the houses.

The Controller frowned and got back inside his helicopter.

'Send Captain Marrs to me at once,' he ordered.

The BEATCON leader swore silently when he saw the Controller arrive. He was furious, but no-one would have known. No-one could ever tell what Captain Marrs was thinking. His dark glasses hid his eyes and no-one had ever seen him smile. Marrs walked over to his helicopter, hardly able to contain his anger.

'Good morning, Marrs,' said the Controller. He looked at the BEATCON leader in his black leather uniform with its famous badge of red lightning on white and the word BEATCON in large red letters. As always, when he actually had to talk to the man, he felt a sense of disgust. Marrs was an evil man. It was a pity that he was so useful. But the Controller was not going to allow him to disturb the life of his own family.

'Is there any reason why you have chosen to come to *these* houses?' asked the Controller. 'You do realise, Marrs, that there are many important people living here who might not enjoy the methods of BEATCON and who might complain to the European Control Centre?' he asked.

Captain Marrs did not move. His expression showed that he was not very worried about anyone who might complain to the European Control Centre. He was a man with a job to do and he was going to do it. He did not mind if he upset people. He looked at the Controller sitting in a comfortable chair in the middle of his own personal helicopter. Like the Controller's office, it was all silver and blue, with blue glass to protect the Controller from the glare of the sun.

Captain Marrs hated the Controller, but there was nothing he could do about it. He knew that it was only because of the Controller that BEATCON existed. Many other people at Control, including the Assistant Controller, wanted to get rid of BEATCON.

'We had information that there were terrorists here,' said Marrs. 'We have destroyed one terrorist.'

'Really?' said the Controller. 'And who was that?'

'His name was Saul Grant,' said Captain Marrs. 'Grant was asking about the Music Rooms.'

'Well, that's not very surprising,' said the Controller. 'Saul Grant was a music critic. A very good music critic.'

'All information about the Music Rooms is secret,' said Captain Marrs. 'If Grant knew about the Music Rooms, then he must have communicated with terrorist groups.'

'I see,' said the Controller. 'And had you thought that Grant might be using the words "music rooms" in a different sense? He probably didn't know anything at all about the real Music Rooms.'

'But he was asking questions,' insisted Captain Marrs. 'Dangerous questions.'

'Oh, very good,' said the Controller. 'So, you've killed a well-known music critic because he asked questions about music. And why have you frightened a group of important old people? What questions have they asked?'

'We think that they are communicating with other known terrorists in Europe. And Grant worked here the day before he began to ask about the Music Rooms.'

The Controller sat back in his soft chair. 'BEATCON is useful, but it exists to hunt terrorists. If it started to think that it had other aims ... if, perhaps, BEATCON thought that it had rather more power than it actually has ... if its leader started to think he was more powerful than Control itself ...' The Controller shut his eyes for a second. Then he opened them again. He stared at Captain Marrs, coldly. 'If BEATCON started to behave like that, I would close it down. In a second. Do you understand?'

Marrs was silent.

'Do you understand me?' asked the Controller. 'You and your men leave here now and you don't come back. Ever.'

'I understand,' said Captain Marrs. He turned and walked back to his jetcar. His face was white. A moment later the BEATCON unit had gone. Inside the jetcar, Dick Lane turned to Captain Marrs.

'We ran a heat scan over the remains of that car, sir,' he reported. 'And it showed nothing. There was no-one inside it. Somebody must have started it up using a remote control unit.'

'I knew it,' said Captain Marrs. 'Someone is playing games with us. Well, Dick, no-one plays games with BEATCON. I don't care who lives in these houses. I don't care if the Controller himself lives there. I want to know everything every one of those old people does. I want to know what they say and what they think. I want to know when they get up in the morning and when they go to bed. I want information.'

'Yes, sir,' said Dick.

Marrs signalled to another member of the BEATCON unit. The young man came up to him.

'That music writer Saul Grant was in those houses on oldie duty. I want you to take his place. Find out who Grant talked to. Search the houses. But don't let anyone know that you're BEATCON. Do you understand?'

'Yes, sir,' said the young man.

'I want information and I want evidence,' said Captain Marrs. 'And I want it now. I'll show the Controller that BEATCON was right.'

'Do you want us to arrange an accident?' asked Dick Lane. 'Perhaps something could happen to the Controller's helicopter.'

'You're a fool, Dick,' said Captain Marrs. 'What do you think would happen next? Well?'

'I don't know,' replied Dick, unhappily.

'Well, think! BEATCON has no place for men who can't think.'

Dick thought. 'The Assistant Controller would become the new Controller?' he suggested.

'Yes. The Assistant Controller would become Controller, and you know what the Assistant thinks of BEATCON, don't you?'

'Yes, sir,' said Dick, wishing he had never spoken. 'He hates BEATCON.'

'If the Assistant Controller became Controller, you'd find yourself out of your uniform and down in the tunnels before you could say "shoot". No. We do not kill the Controller. That is not how BEATCON works. We are here to keep control. Do you understand?'

'Yes, sir,' Dick repeated, thinking that he was now about to be thrown out of BEATCON because of his stupid question.

'Without control there is terrorism,' said Captain Marrs. 'There is terrorism! You don't want terrorism, do you?'

'No sir, of course not, sir.'

'Right. We do not want terrorism, we want order. We want to keep control. And we want to keep BEATCON.' Captain Marrs turned to the rest of his men.

'It seems that this innocent music critic is still alive. But I don't think he is just a music critic. Do you?' he asked.

'No, sir,' his men agreed.

'No,' said Captain Marrs, thoughtfully. 'Music critics do not know how to make their cars move by remote control. I want to find Saul Grant and talk to him. And I want him now!'

Chapter 8 *I never wanted to be a terrorist*

Tuesday 3 June, 9.45 a.m. Richmond Forest.

The tunnel seemed to go on for ever. Saul was tall and had to bend over all the time to stop himself from banging his head on the roof. It was very uncomfortable. His back hurt and he was also colder than he had ever been in his life. He wanted to go home and have a hot shower. Suddenly he realised that he could never go home again. He stopped.

'I've lost my home,' he thought. 'All my things, all the things I've bought over the years, my music collection. I've lost them all. And just because I listened to this woman, Ruth. My life is finished. I might just as well have been inside my car when Captain Marrs blew it up. And it's all Sue's fault. If she hadn't started my car, I could have gone and talked to Captain Marrs and explained everything. And I'd be home now instead of in this awful dark tunnel.'

'What's the matter, Saul?' asked Ruth, behind him. 'Why have you stopped?'

'I've had enough,' said Saul. He was both very unhappy and very angry. He wasn't sure which of the two feelings was the stronger. 'I've lost my home and my job as well, I expect. It's all your fault. I never wanted to be a terrorist. I'm cold and I have no idea where we are or where we're going.'

'I'm sorry about the first things,' said Ruth. 'But it's Captain Marrs you should be angry with, not us. As for

38

where you're going, we're going into the forest. We're nearly there. There's a secret PACE hide-out in a hill in the middle of the forest.'

'You'll really have something to worry about in the forest,' added Sue. 'I bet you've never met any wolves before.'

'She's just saying this to make me feel even worse,' thought Saul. He had never met anyone he disliked more.

'What wolves?' Saul asked. 'What are you talking about?'

'The wolves in the forests,' Sue explained. 'The forests are full of wolves again. Didn't you know that?'

'Is this a joke?' Saul asked Ruth.

'I'm afraid not, dear. It's true. It's because no-one goes into the forests any more. The wolves are dangerous but they usually run off when you shoot at them.'

'Shoot at them!' repeated Saul. 'But I haven't got a gun.'

'I've got a spare one for you,' said Ruth calmly.

'But I've never used a gun before. I wouldn't know how to use one,' argued Saul.

'I told you he was useless,' commented Sue.

'Look here,' said Saul. 'I'm fed up with you saying that. I didn't ask to come here. I'm a music critic and I'm a good music critic. I don't know how to get into other people's Web pages and I don't know how to shoot. People who blow up cars frighten me. Guns frighten me. I'm not a terrorist and I don't want to become a terrorist. I don't like guns and bombs and things. I listened to Ruth because I love dolphin music and I can't bear the thought of dolphins being hurt. I love dolphins. But I hate the thought that I can't go home. At this moment all I want to do is to go home and have a hot shower and listen to some music.

What I really *don't* want right now is to walk out of this tunnel and into a pack of wolves.'

'That's understandable,' said Ruth. 'But I'm afraid there is no alternative. If you went home right now, then Captain Marrs would kill you. And the dolphins would still be in the Music Rooms. You can't go home now. I don't know how BEATCON found out about you, but they did. Otherwise they wouldn't have come to my house this morning.'

'Yes,' said Sue. 'They weren't following me. I spent hours making sure that no-one saw me go to Ruth's house.'

'Yes, I think that may have been my fault,' Saul replied miserably. 'I asked Caroline last night if she'd heard of the Music Rooms.'

'You fool,' commented Sue.

'Oh no!' A new thought had hit Saul. 'Do you think that Caroline is in danger now?'

'I don't know,' said Ruth. 'What did she say when you asked her about the Music Rooms?'

'She said she'd never heard of them. She wasn't even interested.'

'Then I expect she'll be all right,' said Ruth. 'Now, don't worry about Caroline. You just think about yourself. It's not easy to live away from ordinary society. To live away from Control. But it is possible.'

'But you still live in your home,' said Saul. 'Or you did until today,' he added. 'So why are you a terrorist?' It was a question he had asked himself ever since he had first met Ruth.

'I suppose because of Sue,' said Ruth. 'When I found out

what had happened to Sue, I was so angry that I decided to fight Control. So Peter and I set up PACE.'

'What happened to Sue?' Saul was curious.

'It's a long story,' said Sue. She said no more.

Saul continued to think about what Ruth had said. So she wasn't just a member of this group. She was one of the original organisers. That was why she knew so much about other terrorist groups. That was how she knew about the Music Rooms.

'You organised PACE?' asked Saul. 'You and Peter, the Controller's brother. He's PACE as well?'

'Oh yes,' said Ruth. 'Hadn't you guessed?'

'Does the Controller know?' asked Saul.

'That's a very interesting question,' said Ruth. 'I've often wondered, but I've never asked Peter. It wouldn't be fair.' Ruth stopped as light and warmth began to fill the tunnel. 'Here we are, then,' she said.

They all stopped. The tunnel floor had been leading up for some time and Saul realised that they were now in a cave which led directly into the forest. Although it was light compared with the tunnel, it was still quite dark. At least you could walk here without an anti-glare mask, he thought.

They walked out into the forest, looking around them. There was a path from the cave and they followed this. As they walked along, Saul began to smell the forest.

In all the virtual travelling he did there were no smells. But this forest was full of strange smells. There were tree smells, wet smells and earth smells. It was wonderful. Saul wanted to lie down and enjoy the smells all around him. But then, as the wind blew, there was a strange animal smell. It was very strong and it was not at all pleasant.

Then Saul heard it. A wolf howling. On one side and then on the other side of them. Saul had heard it before. There was a virtual journey that he used to enjoy. You travelled in Russia and were chased by packs of wolves. It was very exciting, but you always escaped from the wolves. And if you didn't want them to be there, you could just get rid of them by changing the programme of the journey. But there was no computer controlling these wolves. These were real. Saul was suddenly terrified.

'Take this gun,' said Ruth. 'But only use it when I tell you to. You just press this button to set it and pull the trigger. It's very simple. OK?'

'I'm not sure,' said Saul. 'I'll do my best.'

'You'll do fine,' said Ruth. Saul saw that she, too, was carrying a gun.

'I don't like shooting animals either,' said Ruth. 'But the wolves are very dangerous here. It's a question of us or them. Now keep together,' she added as the sound of the wolves grew louder. 'The wolves are all around us and they may attack at any moment.'

Chapter 9 *Wolves*

Tuesday 3 June, 10 a.m. London.

Dick Lane was fed up. In the past, although he was a special and was part of the unit that went out with Captain Marrs, he had always felt that Captain Marrs did not really know that he existed. Now, for the first time, Captain Marrs had noticed him. And he'd said that Dick was stupid. It wasn't fair. Dick decided that he had to do something to make Captain Marrs pleased with him.

As soon as the jetcar got back from Ruth's house to B Centre, Captain Marrs went up to the Control Room to see whether the satellites had seen anything. He looked down on the houses where his men had been an hour earlier. There was nothing to see. He asked the computer to scan an area of ten miles around the houses. Nothing. Only the forest. And whatever the forest was hiding.

Marrs swore. He hated the forests. He wished that he could burn them all down. But the Controller would not let him do that. The Controller said that the forests were useful: 'If any of our friends in the world should decide to become enemies, Marrs,' the Controller had said, 'we'd need somewhere where we could hide people and weapons. We'd need somewhere where their satellites wouldn't be able to see us.'

The Controller was right, thought Marrs. The Controller thought ahead. That's why he was Controller. But, all the same, thought Marrs angrily, when it came to terrorists, the forests were a major problem.

Dick Lane didn't know why the forests were needed, but he could see that they were a problem. He was looking at a virtual map on his computer and was staring at the same area of forest that Captain Marrs was looking at upstairs, in his Control room. 'The terrorists must be in the forest,' thought Dick. He knew that jetcars could not get into the forest, but a jetbike could.

'We could get into the forest on jetbikes,' Dick thought. 'If Saul Grant and his friends are in the forest, they can't have got very far. I'll kill Grant and Captain Marrs won't say that I'm stupid then.'

Dick did not want any of the BEATCON officers to know where he was going, but he told two of the younger BEATCON soldiers to go with him. Since Dick was a special, they followed him without asking any questions.

Dick had never been inside the forests before, but like Saul, he had travelled through many forests on virtual trips. He thought that it would be the same.

The forest was much darker than Dick had realised, but the jetbikes had excellent lights and Dick was too excited to feel scared. He and the two soldiers shouted to each other as they raced their bikes through the trees.

Then there was a scream. One of the bikes had hit a tree root. In virtual forests, trees did not have roots. The soldier was thrown from his bike, which then fell on top of him. Dick raced up to him, but there was nothing he could do. He was dead.

Dick was not sure what to do next. He and the other BEATCON soldier looked down at the dead boy, shocked and worried. It had all happened so fast. Then they heard the howl. And another one.

'What's that?' asked the second soldier.

'It's a wolf, you fool!' Dick used his anger to hide the fact that he was very frightened. There was another long howl. It was right beside them.

'Get back on your bike!' shouted Dick. 'Let's get out of here!'

Then, in the dark half-light of the forest he saw a huge brown wolf. Dick had never been so scared in his life. He nearly fell off his bike. 'BEATCON men are never scared,' he said to himself. He drew his gun and fired. The wolf fell down dead. Then out of the shadows, between the trees came other wolves, dozens of wolves. They jumped up at him. One of them bit his leg. Dick shot the wolf in the head. He shot at the other wolves again and again. Four more wolves fell down dead.

The other young BEATCON soldier had not yet learned how to ride and shoot at the same time. He found it was very difficult. He lifted his gun and then, a second later, he fell off his bike. Immediately, the wolves were on top of him. Dick drove his jetbike straight at the wolves, shooting crazily, but it was too late. The second soldier was dead, too.

Dick was now terrified. He had lost two BEATCON soldiers and he hadn't even found Saul Grant. All he wanted to do now was to get out of the forest before the wolves killed him, too. He turned round his bike and rode as fast as he could back to B Centre.

Saul, Sue and Ruth heard the shooting and the howls of the wolves. They walked carefully along the path and saw the wolves and the bodies of the two BEATCON soldiers. Saul felt violently sick.

'Should we bury them?' he asked. The wolves were already eating the bodies.

'I don't think there's anything the three of us can do,' replied Ruth. 'I'm sorry, Saul. But the wolves will be less interested in us now.'

They walked on very quietly, their guns ready. Ruth was right, the wolves were not interested. Dick had killed many of them and the rest had enough to eat.

It was nothing like a virtual trip, thought Saul. In virtual adventures, the wolves would have attacked them. But there would not have been any bodies or blood. Or that smell. That terrible smell. Dead wolves and dead men. The real world was horrible. Saul wanted to go back to his safer virtual life. He wanted to go home.

Chapter 10 *Out of control*

Tuesday 3 June, 11 a.m. Richmond Forest.

'I never knew that these forests existed,' said Saul. 'I thought that no-one was allowed to use paper because there were not enough trees. That's what Control said.' Saul looked around him. 'But there are plenty of trees.'

'It's a typical Control lie. You can't believe anything Control says. Control doesn't like paper; paper can be passed from hand to hand without Control seeing it. Control wants everything on the Web where it can be observed.'

'There are forests everywhere in Europe now,' Sue added.

Saul was silent. There was so much to think about. It seemed that everything he had believed was not true. He had been just a part of a huge machine called Control. All the choices that he thought he had made were really very small. His life had been completely controlled, every part of it.

'Why don't more people ask questions?' he asked Ruth finally. 'Why didn't people try to stop Control when it first started to take over?'

'Many people do ask questions,' replied Ruth. 'But most people are happy. They feel safe, their lives are comfortable. Why should they ask questions? The tunnel people do all the real work that is needed to make life pleasant for everyone else. They don't get paid, of course, and they get beaten if they don't work hard enough, and shot if they try to run away. But no-one is ever told about that.'

'Some tunnel people do succeed in running away, though,' added Sue. 'And a few of them live in small communities in the forest. PACE helps them. The largest community is near here. It's run by PACE. And many PACE workers live there. That's where we're going.'

'A community in the forest?' asked Saul. 'But aren't you worried that Captain Marrs will destroy it?'

'Captain Marrs hates the forest,' said Sue. 'His satellites have far less power here. Jetcars can't move in the forest, because there are too many trees, and helicopters can't land here. And this community is hidden in a number of large caves. They are very old and go down deep into the ground. Even Captain Marrs' cameras can't see what goes on in the caves.'

'Captain Marrs did try to get rid of the forests last year,' added Ruth. 'He tried to burn down a forest near London, but the fire very soon was out of control. That was because PACE discovered Marrs' plan. We didn't like burning down the forest but we knew that if we didn't make sure that this fire was huge, then there would be no forests left in England. It's amazing what a little petrol will do,' Ruth added. 'The fire didn't just burn down part of the forest, it also burned down a lot of houses. The Controller was furious. Marrs was told to leave the forests alone.'

'I remember that,' said Saul. 'The fire was blamed on terrorists. Wasn't someone arrested afterwards?'

'Yes,' said Sue angrily. 'But it had nothing to do with them. They were just two tunnel workers that Marrs picked out. They weren't even in England when the fire happened. But Captain Marrs killed them anyway.'

'It's terrifying,' said Saul. 'But isn't there anything anyone can do?'

'Yes,' said Ruth. 'We fight back. That's why we started PACE. But you can't win a war in a day. It takes time.'

They walked on and on. 'My feet hurt,' said Saul, finally. He had never walked much before. Occasionally he did an hour's virtual walking at home, and that was on a rubber mat. The ground was much harder and his shoes were very thin.

'We're nearly there,' said Ruth. 'See that hill there. That's where the caves are.'

Saul had expected to find a few people in the caves, but it was like a small town. There were dozens of caves inside the hill and they were all full of PACE workers.

'You can rest for a few hours now and eat,' said Ruth. 'Then you need to get ready for your journey.'

'What?' asked Saul. He was exhausted. 'I thought we were going to stay here for a while.'

'I'll be staying here,' Ruth told Saul. 'I have a great deal to do. But you're going to Neumatt. Each of us has their job to do and your job is to save the dolphins. We can't waste time.'

'What about the tunnel workers?' asked Saul. 'Someone has to help them, save them.'

'Yes,' agreed Ruth. 'Of course it's important to save the tunnel workers. But it's not *your* job. You've written about dolphin music for so long, now you must rescue the dolphins. Other people will rescue the tunnel workers. And soon, I hope. But you are going to Neumatt. That's why you are here. There's no turning back now.'

Chapter 11 *Find Saul Grant*

Tuesday 3 June, 11.30 a.m. London.

'Now, let me see if I have this correct,' said Captain Marrs to Dick Lane. 'You go into the forest without my permission. You take two BEATCON soldiers without my permission. You take them into the forest, where they are not yet trained to operate. You cause the death of these men. And you fail either to kill or arrest the terrorists. Does that describe your actions this morning? Does that describe the complete disaster of your work this morning? Does it? Are you stupid? Don't you ever listen to me? Don't you think that being a BEATCON special is worth something? Well?'

'I'm sorry, sir,' said Dick, miserably. 'I thought that if I was quick, I might be able to surprise Grant in the forest.'

'You fool. Why didn't you ask me? As an example of a human being you are a disaster. What are you?'

'A disaster, sir,' repeated Dick.

'What makes me really angry,' shouted Marrs, 'apart from the loss of two men, is that I would have said yes. It was a good idea. But I would have sent out a dozen jetbikes, not three. And specials, trained men. But you didn't ask me and now I've lost two soldiers. Is there any reason why I should allow you to remain a BEATCON special?'

'I don't know, sir.'

'I'm a failure,' thought Dick. 'I'm going to be thrown out of BEATCON, perhaps even sent to the tunnels.'

'Next time, I'll kill them all,' he promised.

'Yes, I think you will,' said Marrs. 'Because you will never come back to me again unless they are dead. And that is the only reason that I'm letting you stay on. But I'm watching you, understand? One more mistake and you're out.'

'Yes sir. Thank you, sir.'

'Now get out of here and find Saul Grant. Put out a notice on the Web. Say that Grant is wanted for the murder of the two BEATCON soldiers. Put their pictures on the Web. While you were playing in the forest, I discovered who lived in those old people's houses. It was the grandmother of Sue Hunter. The lovely Sue, she's been on our wanted list for a long time. So put the pictures of Grant and Sue together. Say that they are a dangerous couple who are enemies of Control. Add all the usual things. Later, we can have one of the BEATCON boys' mothers on the Web, crying and asking for information. That's always useful. And make sure that everyone realises that keeping back information about Grant and Hunter is a serious crime. Can you do that?'

'Yes, sir. At once, sir.'

'Good,' said Marrs. 'It won't be long before we find Grant and Hunter. And then they will pay the price for the loss of two of my men.'

Chapter 12   *Night train to France*

Tuesday 3 June, 5 p.m. Richmond Forest.

Saul had thought that he wouldn't sleep. There was so much going on in his mind. But he had been physically exhausted. And the air was so good, so clean. He had never slept outside before.

Before he went to sleep, Saul looked up at the sky and the shapes of the trees. 'It's beautiful,' he thought. The real world was so much more beautiful than the virtual world. Then he remembered the dead wolves. 'It's all very confusing,' he thought. Then he fell asleep. A few hours later, Ruth sent Sue to wake him up.

'This is where we say goodbye,' said Ruth. 'I'm staying here. You and Sue go on without me. I'm needed here.'

Saul was sorry to say goodbye to her. And he wasn't happy at the thought of the journey. He still thought it was a crazy idea and he did not enjoy the idea of travelling with Sue. She was the rudest person he had ever met. But he could see that she knew a lot more than he did about how to exist in this world outside Control.

'What we're going to do,' explained Sue, 'is to join the tunnel workers who are going to France. One of the things that Control does is to move tunnel workers about all the time. They work all over Europe. Moving them around stops the workers getting to know any one place too well.

We need to get out of England quickly. Before Captain Marrs knows that we've gone.'

'How do we do that?' asked Saul.

'We join up with a group when they finish work,' Sue explained. 'But first we have to get ourselves some tunnel clothes and a number.'

'A number?' wondered Saul.

'Every tunnel worker has a number,' Sue told him. 'If people have numbers instead of names, it's easier for those in charge of them to think of them as objects and not as people. If the guards thought that the tunnel workers were people like them, they wouldn't be able to hurt them.'

'Hurt them,' repeated Saul. 'They hurt them?'

'Yes,' answered Sue. 'But they won't hurt us. They only hurt you if you run away or don't work hard enough. The only thing that we'll have to put up with is the heat on the train. It's going to be very uncomfortable, but not too dangerous. Control likes to keep the tunnel workers alive and well. They work better that way. Though if they get really ill, that's it.'

'That's it ... what do you mean?' Saul asked.

'When the tunnel workers get ill or old and they can't work any more, Control sends them down the long tunnel,' Sue explained.

'The long tunnel,' Saul repeated. The words had a terrible sound to them.

'The sick workers walk down the tunnel, thinking that it's the way to a hospital, but then the doors shut and ... well, they die quickly. We think that's what happens, anyway. We're still trying to find out. We think that they are killed underground. And that way, Control doesn't even have to get rid of the bodies. It's very clever.'

'It's terrible,' Saul said. His face was white.

'Yes,' agreed Sue, 'it is. That's why we are trying to stop it all. We're trying to stop all the terrible things that are going on. And that includes the dolphins as well as the people. And we will succeed. In the end. But right now we have to get ready for our trip. And you need a number.'

Sue showed Saul her hand. 'The tunnel workers have their numbers on a small computer chip inside the back of their hand. I've already got one. The guards put it in. But I've changed the number. So they don't know who I am.'

'Did it hurt?' asked Saul.

'It hurt when the guards put it in,' admitted Sue. 'But I'll do yours. I'll rub something into your hand first and you won't feel a thing.'

'How do we reach the tunnel workers?' Saul asked.

'We go into the tunnels,' said Sue. 'The tunnels at the edge of the forest have no guards. The tunnel workers are too frightened of the wolves to escape. Captain Marrs recently decided to keep a few wolves in cages at the edge of the forest. He thought it was useful to show the tunnel workers what happens when a wolf kills a man.'

'He did that?' Saul had thought that the world was a controlled but pleasant place. 'But I never asked any questions,' Saul thought. 'I didn't want to know what went on outside my own house.'

'Yes,' said Sue. 'I told you Marrs was evil. He'll do anything to make sure that no-one questions Control. He's quite mad.'

An hour later Saul and Sue were standing at the

entrance to a work tunnel. They were both dressed in the simple cotton clothes of the tunnel workers and Saul had a small chip under the skin of his right hand. Two PACE workers had guided them through the forest to the tunnel.

'When the day's work is finished and it's time to go back to the houses,' explained the worker, 'that red light there will flash. Then you can walk down the tunnel until you meet the other tunnel workers. Then you follow them. Good luck,' he added.

A few minutes later, the red light flashed.

'That's it,' said Sue. 'Remember, don't tell anyone your real name.' They walked down the tunnel and joined a group of tunnel workers going back to their central building after a day's work in the tunnels. The workers were kept in small groups and moved around all the time so that they could not make close friends. Sue had told Saul that there were PACE members inside many of the groups and it was they who looked after Saul and Sue. Soon they were on the night train going to France.

The night train was an antique from the end of the twentieth century. Once people had paid to travel on it to and from work. Now it was very old and dirty, but it was fast. The night train was one of several trains that took people and goods backwards and forwards between Britain and the rest of Europe.

It was still dark when the train stopped. They had been travelling, Saul estimated, for about six hours. Everyone was told to get out.

'Where are we?' asked Saul.

'I'm not sure,' said Sue.

'Lyon,' said a worker beside them. 'I've been here before. There's a new centre being built here. They need a lot of workers to help with the building.'

'We can't let ourselves become part of a working party,' whispered Sue to Saul. 'We'll never get out. We have to escape now.'

'How?' asked Saul.

'Just do what I tell you,' said Sue. 'I'll get someone to help us.' Saul saw her talk to a tall man with red hair. He nodded.

Sue came back to Saul. 'Wait,' she said.

A minute later, the man with red hair turned to the man beside him and shouted, 'How dare you say that? I'll get you for that!'

'What? What's the matter? I didn't say anything,' replied the other man, quite truthfully.

The man with red hair did not seem to believe him. He punched the other man and knocked him to the ground.

'Sorry,' he whispered, as he leaned over the other man. 'I've got nothing against you, I just have to help someone escape.'

He stood up again and shouted, 'I'll kill you.' The guards ran forward.

'Now!' ordered Sue.

Very quietly she got under the train and Saul followed her. No-one saw them go. The guards were busy trying to grab the man with red hair.

'What will happen to him?' whispered Saul.

'They'll give him a laser beating,' said Sue. 'He's a brave man. But we mustn't think about him. We have to make sure that we get away.'

Chapter 13 *Waiting*

Wednesday 4 June, 9 a.m. Lyon, France.

It was hot. Very hot. Saul thought it was like being inside a fire or a cooking pot.

Saul and Sue sat in a small room in what had once been a house. Now there were only a few walls. A piece of metal made a kind of roof and gave them some shade. Twenty-four hours ago, thought Saul, he had never heard of Captain Marrs. Now he was in France, hiding from the police. Now he was a 'wanted terrorist' and the world he had known no longer existed for him.

As soon as they were inside the room, Sue took out her laptop from the secret pocket in her jacket and called up PACE France.

'It's your niece, Susie,' she wrote in French, knowing that the local anti-terrorist police might be watching the Web. 'I'm in Lyon with my friend. And I need to get back home. Can you help?'

'Your French is very good,' said Saul, watching her admiringly.

'My husband was French,' said Sue.

Saul was about to ask her about her husband when Sue's message was answered.

'Hello Susie, this is Marc,' one of the French members of PACE replied. 'How are you? I'm glad you are well.

Tell me where you are and I'll come and get you. But I'm afraid it will take a while. I'm about five hours from Lyon right now.'

'That's OK,' wrote Sue. 'My friend and I can wait here. How far can you take us? As you know, I live in Neumatt,' she wrote.

'I can't get there. It's too far,' replied Marc.

Saul was watching over Sue's shoulder.

'Ask him if he can take us to Geneva airport,' suggested Saul.

'Why?' asked Sue. But she typed in the question.

'Geneva airport?' replied Marc. 'Yes, that's OK.'

'I've had an idea,' said Saul. 'There's a regular service between Geneva airport and the Neumatt Arts Centre every evening for people who are actually going to the concerts and plays. We could try and get on to that. The last flight leaves about nine, for people going to a late evening concert.'

'That's brilliant,' said Sue. 'Perhaps Ruth was right about you. You aren't so useless after all.'

'But we'll need some proper clothes,' Saul reminded her. 'We can't walk about dressed like this.'

'You're right,' said Sue.

'Marc,' she wrote, 'I can fly home to Neumatt from Geneva, but my friend and I need some smart clothes and the usual.'

'The usual?' asked Saul.

'Papers,' said Sue. 'It's not a word we dare to write. But Marc will know what I mean.'

'Smart clothes are not a problem,' answered Marc. 'Tell me your sizes and I'll bring them. And the usual. I shall leave in about half an hour, but don't give me your exact position until I'm there. You never know who might be reading this. I'm sure your parents always taught you to be careful.'

'That's sensible,' said Sue. 'Marc is cautious, I like that.' She typed in their sizes. 'We look forward to seeing you, Marc,' she added. 'Thanks for everything.'

'Marc, of course, is thinking about the police,' said Sue. 'He sounds nice,' she added.

Saul felt rather annoyed by the last comment but he didn't know why. After all, he was about to ask Caroline to marry him. And he didn't even like Sue, did he?

'Five hours in this oven,' said Saul. 'It's so hot. At least we brought some water with us.'

'Yes,' agreed Sue. 'But we only have one small water bottle each. We must drink it slowly.'

They sat for a while in silence. Then they began to talk quietly to each other. They talked about the things that interested them, the music and films they enjoyed.

'But how did you become a terrorist?' asked Saul. This was what he had wanted to know ever since he met her. 'You weren't always a terrorist, were you?'

'No,' laughed Sue. 'I wasn't born a terrorist. I went to school and got a degree in computer science. Then I got a good job working for the Web. I met a nice man who worked there and we were married. His name was Robert.

'One day Robert was visiting a friend of ours. It was his friend's birthday. But unfortunately his house was next door to the house where a terrorist lived. Captain Marrs thought that Robert was visiting the terrorist. Robert told Captain

Marrs a thousand times that he'd never heard of the terrorist, but Captain Marrs didn't believe him. I won't tell you what he did to Robert, but it was terrible. Then Captain Marrs sent him back to me as a warning. Robert died the next day. I was arrested and put into the tunnels. And that's why Ruth set up PACE,' she added. 'She rescued me.'

Saul watched Sue as she told her story. Sue spoke quietly, but Saul could see how the memories still hurt.

'So Captain Marrs became my number one enemy,' finished Sue. 'And Ruth and I are determined to get rid of him.'

'When did all this happen?' asked Saul.

'About three years ago,' said Sue. 'I've been working for PACE ever since.'

'I'm so sorry,' said Saul. 'I didn't know.'

'That's OK,' Sue smiled. 'How could you know? And I've been hard on you, too. You've been great. Not everyone would give up everything just like that and go off to rescue eight dolphins.'

'I don't think I had a choice, did I?' laughed Saul. 'Captain Marrs blew up my car.'

'I'm sorry,' apologised Sue. 'I shouldn't have moved it like that. It was silly. I was showing off. And it wasn't the kind of thing a music critic would do either. It just made Captain Marrs more suspicious. Mind you,' she added, 'since you'd mentioned the Music Rooms on the Web, Captain Marrs would have shot you anyway.'

'We have to stop this man,' said Saul.

'We will one day,' agreed Sue. 'Now, I'm going to get some sleep. Wake me when Marc says he's nearly here, or if someone arrives.'

She leaned back with her head on Saul's shoulder and fell asleep almost instantly.

Saul sat without moving. It was strange to be so physically close to another person. He could feel her body moving as she breathed. He thought about the life she must have had for the past three years. She could have stayed in the forest and hidden away, but she had decided to fight instead. She was incredibly brave, thought Saul. He realised that he had begun to feel rather fond of her.

Nothing happened all day except it got hotter and hotter. About six hours after Sue first spoke to him, Marc contacted them, then arrived half an hour later.

Marc was nice, but he was also fifty years old and fat, which for some reason pleased Saul a great deal. The clothes Marc brought were perfect. Silk trousers and jackets for both of them, which were cool, comfortable and elegant. Marc had also brought their new identity papers and plenty of food and drink, and also soap and a large container of water, so that Saul and Sue could wash before getting dressed.

Marc also helped them remove the computer chips from their hands.

'You don't want to set off any alarms, do you?' he joked. 'You don't want anyone to think that you're tunnel workers.'

Sue put photographs and eye-scans from her laptop on to the new papers.

'Mr and Mrs Lawrence,' she read out. 'We come from London and work in the Control Centre. We therefore have permission to travel and go to concerts. Excellent. These are really good, Marc. Did you do them?'

'No,' said Marc. 'PACE now actually has someone inside Control Centre who does them for us.'

'That's great,' said Sue. 'More people are joining PACE every day.'

An hour later, full, clean and comfortable, the new Mr and Mrs Lawrence drove off to Geneva in Marc's large air-conditioned jetcar.

Sue booked their places in their new names on the late evening flight to Neumatt as they drove to the airport. They arrived at the airport at about half past eight, half an hour before the flight was due to leave. All airports were now automatic. Computers checked eye-scans and as long as they matched the name on the booked ticket, there were no problems. Within minutes of arriving at Geneva, Saul and Sue were through the computer checks and on the plane, heading for Neumatt.

'It's all gone really well,' said Sue. 'Almost too well. It makes me feel that our luck can't last. Something terrible will happen.'

Chapter 14   *At the Neumatt Arts Centre*

Wednesday 4 June, 9.30 p.m. London.

Captain Marrs was furious. His men were scared.

'Grant and Hunter are in France!' he shouted. 'They went to France last night and you only tell me now?'

'I'm sorry, sir,' said one of his men. 'A woman who was on duty at the station last night saw a couple who looked like Grant and Hunter. The stupid woman has been asleep all day and only switched on her computer this evening before going to work. That's when she called us. She thinks they were on the train that went to Lyon. They could be anywhere by now, of course.'

'Could they, indeed?' asked Marrs. 'Anywhere? Don't any of you remember what Grant said? The Music Rooms. The Music Rooms are in Neumatt. So where are Grant and Hunter going?'

'Neumatt, sir. Do you want me to call BEATCON Switzerland?' he added.

'No, I don't,' said Marrs. 'We are going to Neumatt ourselves. Grant killed two of my men. This is personal. We're going to Switzerland and we're going there tonight.'

Wednesday 4 June, 10 p.m. Neumatt, Switzerland.

From above, the Neumatt Arts Centre looked like a huge white wall of ice.

'It's amazing,' said Saul as the plane came down between the mountains. 'I've been here almost every day of my working life, but the reality is quite different. The evening light on the mountains, it's so beautiful. Virtual travelling isn't the same at all, is it?'

'No,' replied Sue. 'Life is much more exciting.'

Saul laughed. He liked Sue's sense of humour. She was so different from Caroline. And despite everything that had happened to them, he was beginning to enjoy being with Sue. But now he was about to see Caroline. He must stop thinking about Sue.

Now, for the first time in his life, he was going to actually meet Caroline. He was going to be able to kiss her and touch her. Not just her virtual self. He was excited by the thought. She would be so pleased to see him and he could explain it all to her. He was sure that she would understand and help them both.

'Most of the Centre is inside the mountain itself,' Saul told Sue. He had visited the Neumatt Arts Centre with Caroline on the Web so many times that he felt that he knew it quite well. He leaned over Sue's laptop. He could smell Sue's perfume. He had never been so close to a woman before. Sue smelled so warm and exciting. He reminded himself that it was Caroline that he loved.

'Look.' Saul pointed to the plan of the Centre on Sue's laptop. 'The recording studios are here,' he whispered, 'and the Music Rooms must be here. The musicians live in the next block of houses here.'

'OK,' said Sue. 'You go to Caroline first and I'll have a look around. I'll join you in a while. Give her time to get over the shock of seeing you,' she laughed.

Saul found Caroline's house easily. He knocked at her door. She opened it.

'Hello, Caroline! It's me,' he announced.

Caroline was smaller than he had imagined. Saul found that quite a shock, but she was still Caroline, the woman he had looked at nearly every day for the last three years. He held out his arms to her. She stepped back. Caroline had been crying. Her eyes were red.

'Saul!' she said and began to cry. 'What on earth are you doing here? I've just been watching you on the evening news. They said you killed two men. And the police came just now and asked about you. I don't understand. And now you're here. What are you doing here?'

'Can I come in?' This was not what Saul had expected. He had often wondered what would happen when they met for the first time – their first real kiss, sitting together, laughing, holding hands. Saul pushed past Caroline into her house. He was not about to have a discussion outside.

'What do you mean I was on the news? I've never killed anyone. What are you talking about?' Saul asked.

'Oh Saul, I knew it had to be a mistake, but they said it was you. You and some girl. They said you were a couple. Sue someone . . .'

'Sue!' repeated Saul. 'Sue was on the news, too?'

'Then it's true! Who is she?' Caroline said. 'No, don't tell me, I don't want to know.'

'But Caroline ...' Saul took her firmly by the shoulders. 'It's all a lie. Control lie all the time. I'm here because of the dolphins. Sue is helping me. We are not a couple.'

'Dolphins? I don't understand a word you're saying. They say that you're a terrorist,' said Caroline.

'That's ridiculous,' said Saul.

'Is it?' asked Caroline. 'You leave home suddenly. No-one knows where you are and then you come here. And talk about dolphins. But no, I don't think you're a terrorist. I think you're mad!'

'I'm not mad,' Saul said. 'Please, Caroline. Let me explain.'

'Explain ... explain what? I don't want to hear your explanations. Don't touch me!' she screamed as Saul tried to put his arm round her.

'Caroline, please,' begged Saul. 'Listen to me.'

'No,' replied Caroline, angrily. 'I won't listen. I don't understand. Who is this Sue? What are you doing here? I thought I knew you, but ...'

'Please,' begged Saul. 'Just let me tell you what has happened. Then if you still don't believe me, I'll go.'

Saul sat down on the nearest chair and started to tell Caroline everything that had happened. He didn't say very much about Sue, but he told Caroline about the dolphins and about Captain Marrs. And about the tunnels and all the other lies that he had discovered.

'You see,' Saul ended, 'I had to come here and rescue the dolphins. There wasn't anything else I could do. So,' he smiled at her, 'will you help me?'

Caroline looked at Saul in horror.

'I don't believe a word of it,' she said. 'I think you're completely crazy. I'm going to call the police.'

There was a knock at the door.

'That's probably the police now,' said Caroline.

It was Sue. Saul let her in.

'It's her!' shouted Caroline. 'The other terrorist. You *are* a couple. I can see it. I can see it in the way that you look at each other.'

'Caroline, please,' begged Saul. 'I came here because I thought you would want to help.'

'Me?' shouted Caroline. 'Help you?'

'We're not a couple,' said Sue. 'I'm a terrorist, if you like, but your Saul is just here to rescue dolphins. I'm here to help him.'

'Dolphins again,' cried Caroline. 'I can't stand this. You tell me the most terrible things. Things that will give me nightmares and then you ask me to help you. I play the cello. I can't save dolphins.' She looked up. 'Even if half of what you say is true, I still couldn't help you now. You're a wanted man, a terrorist. It's too late.'

'It's *all* true,' said Saul.

Caroline stood up. 'I'm sorry,' she said. 'I don't think that I can believe you. This mad Captain Marrs, dolphins, Music Rooms. It's all crazy. I loved you, Saul, but now I think I never knew you at all. And now I want you both to go. Otherwise I'll call the police.' She turned to Saul. 'I never want to see or hear from you again. Do you understand? I am not calling the police now because I did once love you, but if you ever come here again, I will call them. Now go. Both of you.'

Saul and Sue left Caroline's place quietly. Saul felt sad and angry.

'Why didn't she believe me? I thought she'd understand,' complained Saul.

'Lots of people don't want to know things that frighten them,' said Sue. 'It's easier to believe what Control tells you.'

'But I believed your grandmother,' Saul replied.

'Yes,' said Sue. 'But you're special.'

It was the nicest thing that Sue had ever said to him and Saul felt surprisingly pleased. But he was still upset about Caroline. He leaned against the wall of a tunnel.

'Where do we go now?' he asked Sue. 'We need somewhere to stay until the morning and we obviously can't stay at Caroline's now.'

Sue tapped the keys on her laptop. 'Yes!' she said. 'I've done it. This way,' she told Saul.

'Where are we going?' he asked.

'We're going to the one place where Captain Marrs can't find us,' Sue replied.

Chapter 15   *Rest period*

Wednesday 4 June, 11 p.m. Neumatt.

The Neumatt European Hotel was one of the most modern hotels in the world. It was made of glass which changed colour as people walked past it. Clear walls became dark blue at night and could not be seen through. It was a marvellous hotel and only senior members of Control were allowed to stay there.

'We're in Room 5,' Sue told Saul. 'I've registered us as Mr and Mrs Lawrence. But since our faces are on the news, we'd better go in the back way, through the tunnels.'

Their room had everything. The latest satellite cinema, a huge bed, a sofa and a fridge big enough to walk into. Inside the fridge were bottles of every type of drink anyone could want.

'Wow! So this is how Control live!' exclaimed Sue. 'I've often wondered. And,' she added, 'it's the one place that even BEATCON aren't allowed to come.'

The bathroom was luxurious with a bath the size of a small swimming pool and several bottles of shampoo and sweet smelling soaps.

'I'm going to have a bath,' said Saul, 'oh but I'm sorry, I'm being rude. Would you like to have the first bath?'

'Yes, if you don't mind,' said Sue. 'I don't often get to enjoy a place like this.'

While Sue was in the bath Saul looked around the

rooms of the apartment, then got something to drink from the fridge.

'Do you want something to drink?' he called out to Sue.

'Orange juice will be just fine,' Sue called back. Saul poured out two glasses. He knocked at the bathroom door.

'Come in,' Sue said. She was lying back, covered in bubbles. Saul was suddenly aware of her body and became nervous.

He put the orange juice down near her, then stepped back quickly. Sue noticed he was nervous.

'Would you like to get in?' she asked gently. 'There's plenty of room.'

Saul suddenly found it difficult to breathe and his face went red. But then, looking straight at her, he nodded his head, took off his clothes and joined her in the huge bath.

She threw some bubbles at him and he threw some back. They started laughing and threw more bubbles. He was close to her now, close to her skin. Her smell was clean and fresh. He leaned closer towards her and kissed her.

'You're so warm. Your skin's so soft,' said Saul. 'All these years of virtual relationships and I never knew anything. I never knew that skin was as soft as this or that being with someone could be such fun. The Web's taken away so much, hasn't it?'

'Yes,' agreed Sue. 'Virtual life is useful but you need to meet people and touch people.' She stroked Saul's shoulder. 'And you need to be with people when you laugh. We were not meant to live alone. We are social animals.'

'I thought that people like you were evil,' Saul said. 'I really did think that most people were like me. I thought that they had happy, controlled lives. I even thought that the people who worked in the tunnels had proper houses and got well treated for doing a dirty job. I had no idea … No idea. Like Caroline,' he added thoughtfully.

'And now?' asked Sue.

'Now I just want to change it all. Get rid of Control. Let the people make the decisions.'

'So you want a revolution now,' joked Sue. 'You want to change the world.'

Then she suddenly became serious. 'What about Caroline?' she asked. 'Do you think that the two of you will get together again?'

'I'm not sure if I ever really knew her,' Saul said in a sad voice. 'We speak to each other most days and we have a virtual relationship. But I'd never touched her before today, or ever kissed her. I know you better than I know her. And when I saw her today, it felt strange, it didn't feel right. I sometimes think I'm more in love with her music than with Caroline herself. And I'm not sure if she really loves me either. If she had loved me, she would have believed me. She would have trusted me.'

'It wasn't your fault,' insisted Sue. 'You tried. Don't blame yourself. And now we'd better get some sleep. Tomorrow we have to get up early and try to rescue the dolphins. It's the reason we're here, after all.'

Chapter 16   *Questions for Caroline*

Thursday 5 June, 2 a.m. Neumatt.

There was a loud bang on the door. Caroline looked at her clock. She had not been able to sleep. She kept thinking about everything Saul had said. It had to be crazy, didn't it? Perhaps she should not have been so quick to send him away. She did love him, didn't she? Caroline sat up, red-eyed with tiredness.

There was another bang on the door. It must be Saul again, she thought. Who else would come here in the middle of the night? She didn't know whether she was glad or sorry.

Caroline got out of bed and opened the door, but it was not Saul. It was a tall man in a black leather uniform. On his jacket was the word BEATCON and the famous badge of red lightning.

'You're Caroline Fry?' he said. 'Captain Marrs wants a word with you.'

'Captain Marrs,' thought Caroline. 'Does that mean that Saul was telling the truth? I told him I didn't believe that Captain Marrs really existed. Perhaps I should have listened to him.' Caroline was scared, but she tried not to let the man see it.

'Yes,' Caroline replied angrily. 'I'm Caroline Fry. Why have you woken me up in the middle of the night? Don't you know I have a concert tomorrow?'

'I'm sorry,' said the man, although he did not sound sorry. 'You must come with me.'

'I must?' Caroline raised her eyebrows. 'Don't you know who I am?'

The man sighed. 'If you don't come, then Captain Marrs will come here and he'll be angry. You may think that you're somebody here in Neumatt, but I promise you, you do not want to make our Captain angry.'

'I see,' said Caroline. Her voice was icy. 'In that case I'd better put some clothes on. You can wait outside.'

Captain Marrs had taken over a large room in the Neumatt police station. Caroline looked at the man who Saul had said was the most evil man in the world. Marrs was tall and solidly built. He took off his glasses once and she saw his eyes. They were terrifying. They were cold and without any feeling. 'This man,' she thought, 'is very dangerous indeed.' Saul had been right.

'Sit down,' demanded Captain Marrs.

Caroline sat down. The questioning began. Caroline decided that whatever she now thought, she should make herself sound stupid. As if her only world was music.

'What did you tell Grant about the Music Rooms?' asked Captain Marrs.

'Nothing,' answered Caroline, making her voice sound surprised. 'How could I? They don't exist, do they?'

'Have you spoken to Saul Grant since that conversation?' he asked.

'Yes,' said Caroline. She looked at a clock on the wall. 'I spoke to him about four hours ago.'

'Did he say where he was?' asked Captain Marrs.

'He didn't have to say where he was,' replied Caroline.

'He was in my room. He came into my room and started trying to talk to me. There was some woman with him. I told them both to go away.'

'What did he tell you?' asked Marrs. 'Did he say where he was going?'

'He didn't say anything,' lied Caroline. 'I wouldn't let him speak. I was very angry with him. He didn't come to my last concert. And then to arrive suddenly when I've got a concert tomorrow. I need to be quiet before a concert. He knew that. And how dare he bring another woman with him! No,' Caroline said, 'I didn't let him say a word. I shouted at him and told him to go away. And I meant it. I never want to see him again.'

'Why didn't you call the police when Saul Grant came to your room?' asked Captain Marrs. 'Didn't you know he was wanted for murder? Didn't you see it on the news this evening?'

'The local police told me that they were looking for Saul,' replied Caroline. 'They told me that Saul had disappeared. And I don't watch the news. I was getting ready for my concert. I don't think you understand about musicians, Captain. We need complete peace and quiet before a concert.'

'I see,' said Captain Marrs. He had never met anyone like Caroline before. He didn't like her, but he believed her. It seemed that she was only interested in her music. She was obviously not a terrorist.

'May I go now?' enquired Caroline. 'I have a concert in a few hours and I must get some sleep.'

'He believes me,' she thought.

'Yes. You can go.' Captain Marrs smiled. It was not a

pleasant smile. 'If it's of any interest to you, we tried to arrest Grant and the woman an hour ago,' he lied. 'But they started to run, so we had to shoot them. Grant is dead.'

'Don't show your feelings, don't let him know what this means,' said Caroline to herself.

'I see,' she said, coldly. 'Then you don't need me at all.'

Back in her room Caroline lay on her bed, crying. Saul was dead and she hadn't believed him. She could have saved him, she thought. Now it was too late. But there was still something she could do. In memory of him. So that his death would never be forgotten. She shut her eyes and tried to remember everything that Saul had said to her. Because of her musical training she could always remember conversations. She lay quietly and let Saul's voice play in her head, like a recording.

'No, Saul,' she whispered. 'No-one will ever forget you after tomorrow.'

Chapter 17   *Get the dolphins out*

Thursday 5 June, 5 a.m. Neumatt.

'Grant is here in the Neumatt Centre,' Captain Marrs told his specials after speaking to Caroline. 'I want him found. Do you all understand? I want him found now!'

The specials all studied their computers and searched every corner of the Neumatt Arts Centre. Every building had its own hidden cameras. Except one.

The Neumatt European Hotel did not allow hidden cameras. Because only senior Control managers were allowed to stay in the hotel, no cameras were allowed in the rooms.

Saul and Sue were asleep, safe in the hotel. Not one of the BEATCON men could find them. The specials looked down every corridor, in every tunnel and in every room in the Centre, except for the hotel rooms. And they found nothing.

'He's there, somewhere,' said Marrs. 'He's clever this one. But no terrorist can trick BEATCON. We'll get him and that Hunter girl. Keep watching the screens. And as soon as you see anything, call me.'

Hours went by. The men grew tired of watching the screens. Empty rooms, empty tunnels, empty corridors. It was very boring, they thought. They wanted to be out there, somewhere, doing something. They hated screen-watching. At five o'clock in the morning, Captain Marrs went out to talk to the local police. His men relaxed a bit.

'How long are we going to do this?' groaned Dick Lane.

'You'll probably be on screen duty all day after what happened in the forest,' laughed one of the older specials.

'It's just too big, this Neumatt Arts Centre,' Dick complained.

'I know,' agreed his colleague. 'So let's be clever. Behave like Captain Marrs always tells us to behave. Think like a terrorist. What do terrorists do? They hide bombs. They interrupt recordings. So what should we watch? All the recording studios and the tunnels under the main buildings. Those are the places Grant is most likely to go. Right?'

'Right,' the men agreed. They fixed their screens on the underground areas and then sat back and relaxed. Grant probably left last night, they thought. This is just a waste of time.

As the BEATCON men talked and watched, on the other side of the Centre, in their hotel room, Saul and Sue were waking up. Saul wondered whether he should call Caroline, but decided that he would wait until he had rescued the dolphins.

Sue looked at a plan of the Centre on her laptop to work out the quickest route to the Music Rooms from their hotel room.

'What's that?' asked Saul, pointing to a line on the plan.

'It's an old railway line,' said Sue.

'Do you think that if we can get the dolphins from the Music Rooms to there, we can transport them out on the trains?' Saul asked.

'Well, my guess is that they're electric trains,' Sue said, 'built about twenty or thirty years ago, before wind power and jet power took over. If we can find the source of the electricity and turn it on, then yes, why not. I'll check on the laptop. But let's find the Music Rooms first.'

The Music Rooms were easy to find. The eye-scanner accepted Saul's eyes and the doors opened. It was silent inside except for the sound of the electricity. Saul and Sue walked into the rooms slowly. Inside eight small glass tanks were the dolphins. They lay without moving and there were electric wires attached to them.

'We're too late,' said Saul. 'They're dead.'

'I don't think so,' said Sue. 'They've been given drugs.'

'We have to turn off the electricity before we move them,' said Saul, 'or we'll be electrocuted.'

Sue found a switch and turned it off. Then she and Saul took all the electric wires off the dolphins.

'OK,' said Sue. 'Give me a moment to look on my laptop. Why don't you go and calm the dolphins?'

Saul walked over to a computer and switched it on.

'Eye-scan,' said the screen. Saul looked into the eye-scanner.

'Accepted,' said the computer. 'Good morning. What can I do for you?'

'I'd like some sea music,' said Saul.

'Rough sea, quiet sea, summer sea, seagulls – which sea music do you want?' asked the computer.

'Oh, I don't know,' said Saul. 'Quiet sea, I think.'

A moment later the room was filled with the sound of waves on a beach. It was quiet and restful. Saul walked over to the dolphins. Their names were on the sides of their tanks. The first was Wind, the dolphin whose music he had listened to only a few days before.

'I don't know if you can understand me,' Saul told the dolphin, 'but we'll get you to the sea, I promise you.'

'Yes!' said Sue in delight. 'We're in luck. There is a train down there and the system is really easy to work. With any luck I should be able to programme it to take us all the way to Italy. And there's a lift to the trains just near that door.' She pointed to the far end of the room.

'You're brilliant,' Saul said. He walked over to the lift and began to think. 'We can only get about two dolphin tanks into the lift at a time. That means four trips. So I'll start getting these poor dolphins out of this horrible room and down to the railway straight away.'

'We should be OK for time,' said Sue. 'There won't be anyone coming here for an hour or more.'

Saul spoke gently to the dolphins as he took them down to the train. It was a large train with big trucks that had once been used to carry machines and other heavy things. There was plenty of room for the dolphin tanks.

Sue helped Saul wheel the heavy tanks along the platform and on to the train. It was hard work and by the time the last dolphin was on the train, they were both exhausted.

'Right,' said Saul. 'Let's go!'

Chapter 18 *On the train*

Thursday 5 June, 6.30 a.m. Neumatt.

When Captain Marrs returned to the room in the Neumatt police station, the BEATCON men went back to their previous search of the entire Centre. The young special watching one of the screens was so used to seeing empty tunnels that he almost missed the sight of Saul and Sue who were putting the last dolphin on to the train. He looked closer.

'It's Grant, sir!' he shouted. 'Tunnel 00987, train station camera 3,' he added.

Every BEATCON screen was switched to this camera.

'What are Grant and the woman doing?' asked Dick.

'Putting something on the train,' said Marrs. 'Probably a bomb. We've got him. You, you and you,' he pointed. 'Come with me.' Marrs grabbed his laser gun. 'This time we've got them. You,' Marrs pointed at Dick. 'You stay here and watch the screens. There may be others with them.'

On the train Saul was making sure that all the dolphin tanks were safely tied on. Sue had found an electricity source and turned it on. Now she was studying the plan of the railway line on her laptop.

'There are lots of bends,' Sue said. 'We mustn't go too fast or the water will pour out.'

'I'll watch the dolphins,' suggested Saul. 'And I'll make sure that they don't get dry,' he said.

'No, I'll do that,' said Sue. 'I want you to drive the train.'

'What?' gasped Saul. 'But I've never driven a train before.'

'It's just like a jetcar,' replied Sue. 'Just drive along the rails and make sure you don't hit anything. I've put the journey into the train's computer, so all you have to do is turn the switch on and go.'

'OK,' agreed Saul, doubtfully.

He climbed into the front of the train and turned on the switch. Dozens of lights and numbers flashed up on the screen in front of him. He didn't understand any of them. There seemed to be a brake, and a pedal which made the train go faster or slower.

'I'm ready,' he called.

'OK,' said Sue.

At that moment they heard the sounds of feet running towards them.

'Go!' screamed Sue. 'Go! Go!'

Saul lifted the brake and pressed the pedal. The train moved forward.

'Faster!' screamed Sue.

Saul pressed his foot down hard on to the floor. The train moved along a bit faster.

A laser flashed through the train and just missed his head.

'Get down!' screamed Sue, who was now lying on the floor beside the dolphins. 'It's Captain Marrs.'

Saul made himself as low as he could and kept his foot on the pedal.

'Get me a train!' shouted Captain Marrs as Saul and Sue's train disappeared down the tunnel.

Sue walked through the carriages of the train. The dolphins lay very quietly in their tanks.

'What have they done to you?' thought Sue. She splashed a little water on each one of them and stroked them.

'I know you can't understand me, but no-one's going to hurt you again. You're going back to the sea,' she told them. The dolphins did not move.

'Perhaps,' thought Sue, 'they think they are already swimming in the sea.' She walked up the train to see whether Saul was all right.

'Yes, I'm OK,' he replied. 'And we made it, didn't we?'

'Don't speak too soon,' answered Sue. 'Look at your screen. We're being followed.'

Saul looked down at the screen, which showed his train as a white dot on a green line. A few minutes ago the train they were on had been the only white dot. Now another white dot was following them. And it was moving faster than they were.

'I hate to say this,' said Sue, 'but that's Captain Marrs. He's got another train and he's coming up behind us.'

'What are we going to do?' asked Saul. 'I can't go any faster because of the dolphins.'

'I know,' said Sue. 'We'll have to stop him.'

'How do we do that?' asked Saul.

'We close the tunnel,' said Sue. 'Now I want you to go as fast as you can for one minute and then stop. I'll make sure that the dolphin tanks are OK.'

'But won't Captain Marrs' train hit us?' wondered Saul.

'No,' said Sue. 'It won't come close, Saul,' she added as Saul was about to object. 'Think about who I am, what I do.'

'What do you mean?' asked Saul.

'I'm a terrorist, aren't I? It's what you've been saying ever since we met.'

'I'm sorry,' said Saul. 'I didn't mean to be rude . . .'

'You were right,' Sue replied. 'I am a terrorist. Captain Marrs turned me into a terrorist. Now think. What do terrorists do?'

'They make bombs,' said Saul slowly. 'You're not going to blow up the tunnel, are you? How?' he added. 'We haven't got a bomb.'

Sue opened her bag. 'Not quite true. *You* haven't got a bomb.'

Saul was shocked. 'You mean you've been carrying a bomb around all this time! Even in the hotel. It might have blown us up.'

'Don't be silly,' said Sue. She sounded, thought Saul, just as she did when he first met her.

'It won't blow up until I set it to blow up. It's a very small, very clever little bomb and it's just what we need. Now can you do what I ask?'

'I suppose I have to,' complained Saul. 'But I don't like the idea. You will be careful,' he added.

'I'm always careful,' replied Sue. 'And it's our only hope.'

Saul put his foot down hard on the pedal and the train speeded up. And so, he noticed, did the train behind them. Then, one minute later, he pulled the brake hard. The wheels of the train screamed as the train came to a sudden stop. Saul watched the white dot which was the train bringing Captain Marrs and BEATCON closer and closer.

Sue had jumped out and was placing something in the middle of the line.

Saul watched the white dot of the approaching train. It was so close that he thought he would see the train at any moment.

'Go!' shouted Sue. Saul pressed the pedal and the train began to move forward again. Sue jumped back on to the train. It began to move faster.

'Get down!' shouted Sue. 'Now!'

There was a huge explosion and the tunnel behind suddenly disappeared. All Saul could see was black smoke.

'Yes,' shouted Sue and Saul together.

'We've done it!' shouted Sue. 'We've killed Captain Marrs!'

Chapter 19 *Surprise for Captain Marrs*

Thursday 5 June, 7 a.m. Neumatt.

Captain Marrs watched the screen in his train. His train was going faster that the one in front, and he knew that in a few minutes he would catch the terrorists. His train was getting closer and closer to the train in front. Then the train in front suddenly stopped.

'What's happening?' asked one of his men. 'What are they doing?'

'Stop!' shouted Captain Marrs. 'Stop the train! They're bombing the line!'

His train slowed, its brakes screaming, and stopped. At that moment, just in front of them, there was a huge flash and the tunnel exploded.

'Another few metres and that would have been us,' said a young BEATCON special. He looked at the blocked tunnel ahead of them. 'Another minute and we would all have been dead.'

'Go back!' shouted Captain Marrs, his face white with anger. 'We'll get them from the air when they come out of the tunnel. It's not over yet!'

'I can't get a signal in this tunnel,' complained Sue, a few minutes later. 'We're too deep. I need to tell the PACE group in Italy where we are. I didn't dare to do it yesterday in case their Web sites were being watched. But we'll need their help when we get out of the tunnel and into open countryside.'

'I thought we were safe now,' said Saul, watching the line ahead and driving carefully along the dark tunnel. 'You said that we'd killed Captain Marrs.'

'I thought I'd blown up his train,' said Sue. 'But you haven't been watching the screen, have you? He stopped his train in time.'

'But the tunnel is still blocked, isn't it?' asked Saul.

'Oh yes,' replied Sue. 'Marrs has gone back to the station. But he's going to be even more determined to get us now. He will probably attack us from the air.'

Saul slowed the train. 'But what are we going to do? We can't just stay inside the tunnel. He's bound to hit us as soon as we get out of the tunnel.'

'Maybe he will, maybe he won't,' said Sue. 'Even after we get out of the tunnel, we're still in a deep valley between the mountains. It will be very difficult for his helicopters to reach us.'

'But we have to leave the valley at some point,' argued Saul.

'Yes,' agreed Sue. 'But we can choose where that will be.'
She studied a map.

'As soon as we get out of this deep tunnel, I can get a signal and use my laptop again,' she said.

The train travelled on and on in the dark tunnel, and then suddenly they saw light ahead of them.

'Now,' Sue told Saul, 'slow down here and try and stop just at the end of the tunnel.'

The train slowed and stopped. Sue tapped away on her laptop, frowning hard. Then she smiled.

'We've got a chance,' she said.

'Did you manage to reach the Italian PACE group?' asked Saul.

'Yes,' said Sue. 'There's a big group near Turin, not so far from here. And they have a great deal of army equipment. When Captain Marrs arrives, we'll be waiting for him.'

The next hour was slow and frightening. The train moved out of the tunnel and along the narrow valley. From time to time Saul and Sue could see the flash of sun on metal; they knew that there were helicopters above them, that they were being watched.

'Marrs is very clever,' said Sue. 'He's prepared to wait. He knows that we will soon be out of the mountains. I think I know just where he will attack us.' She pointed to her laptop.

'There's a short tunnel here which comes out by this river. And there the valley is wide and flat. That's where he's going to wait for us. I'll tell the group to meet us there.'

'But what if the PACE group can't get there in time?' asked Saul.

'Then we wait in the tunnel until they arrive. It's the dolphins we have to think about. They've suffered enough already.'

It was another hour before their train reached the tunnel beside the river. Saul thought that if he wasn't so frightened he would be able to admire the views. It was very beautiful countryside. And he realised now that virtual travel was quite different from real travel. No wonder, he thought, that old people weren't interested in virtual journeys. Virtual journeys were not much more than films. Being there was so much better.

He took the train very slowly through the tunnel and stopped just before the end. Sue jumped out.

'Stay and make sure that the dolphins are OK,' she said. 'I'll see if there's anyone out here.'

She walked to the end of the tunnel. Saul could see her against the light. She looked so small. He was scared for her. Then he heard voices.

'It's OK!' Sue shouted back to him. 'Marrs is not here yet. But the PACE group are here, and Marc, too. And they've got lots of guns!'

'Can I help?' asked Saul, jumping down off the train. He met Marc who was with a large Italian man, carrying guns.

'Well done!' the Italian man said. 'You bring us BEATCON and we'll kill them.'

'Thank you ...' began Saul, but he did not have the chance to say any more. The man was too busy setting up his guns. Saul saw that there were other guns, too, in the trees by the river.

'Marrs will see us, of course,' Sue told Saul. 'His helicopters have the latest satellite cameras. But he won't be expecting all of this. It's our turn to surprise him.'

Chapter 20 *Caroline alone*

Thursday 5 June, 1 p.m. Neumatt.

Caroline was getting ready for her concert. She had put on her favourite dress and made up her face carefully. She was going to be playing alone, without the orchestra, and the concert would be live on the Web.

Caroline began with one of her favourite pieces, by Mozart, but as she came to the end of the music, she played more quietly and began to speak.

'I am playing this work for my friend Saul Grant, the writer,' she told her worldwide audience. 'Saul Grant was a wonderful man, but he died earlier today. Before he died, he discovered that here in Neumatt a terrible thing was going on. The dolphin music that you and I, and all of us, have enjoyed is not natural. The dolphins are hurt with electricity in a place called the Music Rooms and they create this music only when they are dying. Because Saul wanted to stop this, BEATCON called him a terrorist and killed him. Saul was not a terrorist. And these are the other things which Saul discovered before he died ...'

All over the world the audience, which had been listening to the concert as a background to other activities, stopped what they were doing and listened to Caroline. They called their friends and more and more people switched on the Web to hear her.

'Saul is dead, but I am here to tell you that Control lies to you. They lie about the dolphins, they lie about the tunnel workers. Workers, like the dolphins, are being hurt and killed every day. We don't ask questions because most of us don't want to hear these things. I didn't want to. But someone has to start asking questions. Someone has to stop BEATCON killing innocent people. I realise that I may be in danger because I'm saying this ...'

As she spoke, the door of the recording studio opened and before Caroline could say another word, Dick Lane fired three times, straight at her, then said: 'No mistakes this time. This time I found the terrorist and I shot her.'

Caroline fell down, dead, beside her cello. It was a sight that was sent around the world on every computer screen.

In the studio the picture of Caroline was quickly replaced by a picture of a snow-covered mountain.

'We apologise to all of you who were looking forward to that concert,' a voice said. 'And now, until our next programme, here is some music.'

'What has happened to Caroline Fry?' everyone asked each other. 'Is it true what she was saying?'

Control quickly published a statement on the Web.

'We regret the death of the popular musician Caroline Fry,' said the statement. 'But we have discovered that Caroline Fry was a terrorist. She worked with the terrorist Saul Grant. The things said by Miss Fry are not true. We regret that her death may have upset some people.'

'That should be enough,' thought the Controller. 'People forget things so quickly. Caroline will be forgotten in a day or two.'

But the sight of Caroline being murdered as she spoke was not easily forgotten and many people now began to ask the questions that she had asked.

Thursday 5 June, 1.30 p.m. Italy.

Saul knew nothing of Caroline's death. He sat on the train and waited. It was very quiet, thought Saul. There was just the sound of a few birds in the trees. He decided to go and talk to the dolphins and make sure that they were safe.

Then he heard the sound of the helicopters. There were two of them and they came very fast. Even before they reached the tunnel they began to fire. There was a flash at the end of the tunnel and Saul was knocked to the ground. He got up and managed to get inside the train. The dolphins were splashing around in their tanks in terror.

'It's OK,' Saul said softly. But then another explosion hit the tunnel itself just behind the train and the train shook.

In the air above the tunnel, the helicopter pilot wanted to turn back.

'We don't stand a chance against all these guns,' he said. 'Why don't we go back and fetch the army?'

'Never!' screamed Captain Marrs. 'This is my battle. It's us or them!' he shouted. 'Bomb them all! Kill them!'

In the tunnel, the noise grew louder and louder as the terrorists fired back. It was quite different from a film, thought Saul. It was noisy and uncomfortable and he couldn't see anything. He had no idea what was happening. All he could see was the dark of the tunnel and flashes as guns were fired. Then there was a terrible crash and part of the tunnel fell on to the train just beside him. Bits of metal flew around and Saul felt a pain in his arm. There were two huge bangs and then he remembered nothing else.

Chapter 21   *Dolphin sunset*

Thursday 5 June, 1.45 p.m. Italy.

'Saul! Saul! Are you there?'

There were bits of brick and bits of metal covering him. Saul tried to move. His right arm hurt. He touched it. It was wet and he realised that it was bleeding.

'Sue!' he tried to say, coughing with dust.

'Saul!' It was Sue and now she was there beside him, her arms around him.

'Thank heavens you're alive,' she gasped. 'I was so scared. I thought that they'd killed you.'

'Captain Marrs?' asked Saul.

'He's dead,' said Sue. 'This time he really is dead. Both the helicopters were blown up. But three of our people died, too.'

'What about the dolphins?' asked Saul, trying to stand.

'Stay there,' ordered Sue. 'Don't move. You're bleeding.'

'It's just my arm,' said Saul.

'I'll get a bandage,' said Sue. 'But, first, I'll see how the dolphins are.'

She came back a minute later. 'Most of them are fine,' she told Saul. 'There's just a lot of dust in the water. But Wind has been hit. He's badly hurt.'

'Oh no,' said Saul. 'What can we do?'

'I don't think we can do anything,' said Sue. 'We just need to get them to the sea as soon as possible.'

'How?' asked Saul. 'The train's finished.'

'I'll talk to the group,' Sue replied. She came back a moment later with another woman.

'This is Sofia,' Sue told him. 'She's one of the fighters who saved us.'

'Marc has gone to get lorries,' Sofia told Sue. 'They will take you to Genoa. But later. In the day it's too hot and maybe people are looking for the helicopters.'

'I'm not sure about that,' said Sue. 'I have a feeling that Captain Marrs was working on his own.'

'Good,' said Sofia. 'Then I'll leave you. Here are water and bandages. The lorries will be here before it gets dark.'

Saul and Sue spent the rest of the day trying to clean the water in the dolphin tanks and talking quietly to the dolphins. They were very worried about Wind. He did not move and his eyes were shut.

Just before the sunset, they heard a strange noise they had never heard before. It got louder and louder. Eight lorries appeared. Saul and Sue looked at them in disbelief. They had never seen anything like them.

Marc jumped down, laughing. 'They're great, aren't they? They are old petrol-driven lorries. They belonged to Sofia's great-grandfather. But they still go. And there will be enough room for you and the dolphins. Now,' he added, 'let's get these dolphins of yours safely inside. Then we go to Genoa.'

Saul and Sue sat in the last lorry with Wind. He was badly hurt and they worried that he would die before they reached the sea.

As they drove along, Sue began as usual to tap into her computer.

'There's an urgent message from Ruth!' she exclaimed. 'She wants us to watch the news.'

Sue tapped again. To their surprise there was a picture of Caroline and then they saw the Controller's brother, Peter, sitting at a desk.

'... And because of that,' Peter was saying, 'the Controller has resigned and I am now your new Controller.'

'What!' exclaimed Sue and Saul together.

Peter was now replaced by a newsreader. 'The murder of the brilliant, young musician, Caroline Fry, is today's top news story,' he said.

'Caroline murdered,' whispered Saul.

'It appears that the man who killed her was working for BEATCON and carrying out the orders of its leader, Captain Marrs.

This evening the death of Captain Marrs has been confirmed and the new Controller has promised that in future the powers of BEATCON will be reduced.

The new Controller has also promised early elections and a freer society. More news follows this announcement.

This has been an extraordinary day for the world. It was a day which began with the brutal death of Caroline Fry, watched by millions on the Web. Caroline Fry died to honour the memory of music critic Saul Grant who, we have been told, was not a terrorist or a murderer as previously announced. It was thought that Grant was dead, but we have just heard that Grant may still be alive. We will bring you news of this as soon as we get it.

We leave you for a moment with the sound of Caroline playing her favourite work, the Bach cello suite.'

As the music played, tears ran down Saul's face.

'She died for me,' he said. 'She was so brave. She did love me. I was wrong. And now it's too late.'

'She died for all of us,' said Sue, crying herself. 'And she's done what none of us could do. She's forced the Controller to resign. It's all over. We're not in danger any more.'

The lorries slowly drove through the night, through the empty landscape of northern Italy. Saul sat silently thinking about Caroline. Sue watched him, wondering what she would do when they got back home and whether Saul would be a part of her future life.

It was almost morning when they reached the sea. The lorries drove on to the beach. Marc opened the door and the smell of the sea filled the lorry. Wind moved in his tank.

'Not long now,' said Saul. 'Just give us a few moments to get you into the water.'

Saul's arm was very painful and he could not do very much, but Marc and his friends got the tanks off the lorries and into the sea. As soon as the water covered the dolphins, they realised that they were free and swam away fast.

Wind was the last dolphin to be released. He could not move so Saul and Sue pushed him into the water. Then Saul walked out into the sea and swam a little way out, pushing the sick dolphin gently before him.

The other dolphins jumped and swam in the water. Then, suddenly, they all swam back to Wind. Very gently, the seven other dolphins pushed the injured dolphin out to sea with them.

In the distance the sun was beginning to rise above the water and, in the faint early morning light, Sue and Saul heard the most wonderful sounds.

It was Wind. The dying dolphin was singing his last song. Free once again, Wind created the last piece of dolphin music that anyone ever heard. And it was the most beautiful music ever created.